Looking for Miss Sargam

Looking for Miss Sargam

Stories of Music and Misadventure

SHUBHA MUDGAL

SPEAKING TIGER

SPEAKING TIGER PUBLISHING PVT. LTD
4381/4, Ansari Road, Daryaganj
New Delhi 110002

First published in hardback by Speaking Tiger 2019

ISBN: 978-93-88874-88-5
eISBN: 978-93-88874-89-2

10 9 8 7 6 5 4 3 2 1

Typeset in Adobe Jenson Pro by SÜRYA, New Delhi

For Jaya and Skand Gupt—my parents and first gurus—who taught me the alphabet, sargams, storytelling and more.

Contents

Aman Bol

At first glance, Shweta Bansal did not look like she belonged in her air-conditioned office in the heart of Mumbai. Sallow, nearing forty and dressed in a flashy, distracting palazzo-kurta set, she seemed to have tumbled out of a Hindi soap opera. She had a hopped-out-of-bed-and-ran-to-office look—unkempt hair, slightly puffy eyes, and hands unsteady from too little sleep and too much coffee. But when she spoke, there was nothing diffident about her at all; she was so confident, she was brash.

Her conversational style, though, was about as chaotic as her appearance. As she spoke now to the man sitting across her desk, her voice filled the room in hurried, jumbled bursts that were interrupted every few minutes by one of her two cell phones ringing stridently. The ringtone on one played 'Desi Boyz'; on the other, the Gayatri Mantra. Before she answered each call, she would ask her guest hurriedly, 'Sorry, may I take this call for just a sec?' And without further ado, she would begin talking: barking out orders to a junior; speaking in falsely respectful tones to an important caller; rolling her eyes heavenwards in exaggerated disgust talking to someone who was no longer useful but had to be suffered because you never knew...

Disconnecting, she would return to the business at hand, which entailed coaxing Sikander Sufi, one of the leading playback singer-composers of the country, to be part of a mega event that she was planning. Pleasant, portly, and hugely successful, Sufi took each of Shweta's calls in his stride, as he did her sales pitch about the concert—never committing but never refusing outright either, while the woman changed her stance and her strategies with practiced ease.

At thirty-eight, Shweta was Vice President, Marketing and Events of Media Mines, the company that owned, among hundreds of other assets, the country's once most prestigious and currently most successful daily, *The New New Times* (TN2T) published simultaneously from fifty-one cities. It had the distinction of having set new standards and trends in selling every inch of space. It was no longer just ad space that was on offer; you could now buy a story, a column, a feature on any activity you wished to indulge in, even if it was nose-picking in public or picking fluff from your lover's navel. And of course, if you were seriously loaded you could buy the entire front page, masthead and headlines too. At the helm of the team trading in media space was Shweta Bansal, garishly dressed, messy, but tolerated because she could rake in sacks of moolah for Media Mines. She had earned her brashness, every column inch of it.

But it wasn't Shweta Bansal alone who dripped arrogance, cunning and hypocrisy in turns. Sikandar Sufi was no babe in the woods, either. Born Sikandar Liddar in Punjab's Moga town, he had inched his way to Mumbai armed with little other than a magnificent singing voice that could stop you dead in your tracks as it soared, surged, swooped, dipped and did somersaults effortlessly. He had been a bit of a child prodigy, and had started out by singing in orchestra parties with his parents, wearing brightly coloured bhangra costumes in satin, lovingly stitched by his mother on the pedal-operated sewing machine that had been part of her dowry. By the time he was twenty, Sikandar was in demand across Punjab, performing at every kind of gathering, from wrestling tournaments to NRI bashes. His renditions of the Sufi poet Waris Shah's *Heer* moved grown men to tears, and when he sang at weddings, arthritic grandmothers began to dance. But the big break was a long time coming—it was a full six years after he began to cultivate a local politician, singing at the man's election rallies and binge-drinking parties for free, that he recorded his first album, and another three years before a Bollywood producer discovered him. From there, it had been a steady climb.

Somewhere on the journey from Moga to Mumbai, Sikandar Liddar had discarded the satin and the surname. He had chosen a judicious mix of silk and cotton, and renamed himself Sikandar Sufi, a name he could retain as long as Sufi music remained fashionable—in other words, for at least a hundred years. With the new surname and wardrobe came an all-new image: here was a metrosexual mystic musician, with designer stubble, kaajal-lined eyes and sweeping tresses styled and blow-dried to perfection. His hair, in fact, was a living thing on stage, especially when he whipped his head around to the soulful beats he was selling his fans. Flowing black or deep-blue garments, prayer beads worn carelessly around his neck and left wrist, a copper band around his right ankle, all added to the mystic magic of Sikandar Sufi.

For there were thousands of good musicians, hundreds of good voices, so you needed more than plain talent; you needed to be a little different, you needed to be photogenic, you needed to be practical—reading the wind and shifting loyalties with great finesse—and then you could live the life you had always dreamed of. Here, Shweta knew, was an artiste who could match her moves with street-smart dexterity.

'Sikandar yaar,' she cooed, 'that new song you've done for Yashji's new film is simply awesome ya! "*Itne akele...*" It's tooo much yaar, I can't stop playing it in my car!'

Bowing his head slightly, and holding a ringed and bejewelled hand to his heart, Sikandar Sufi acknowledged Shweta's fulsome praise.

'Magical,' Shweta continued, sensing she had made an impact. 'No one can touch you ya! Just watch out for evil eyes. *Nazar utarwaa le yaar, sachchi bolti hoon.*'

Now Sikandar moved his hand lightly, ever so lightly, to his right ear, shutting his eyes for a moment, opening them to gaze heavenwards. His chest heaved, and with arms outstretched and raised towards the sky beyond the false ceiling, he exclaimed, '*Maula, tere karam Maula!* (Your blessings, Lord!) *Maula kasam Shwetta, merko aaj tak ye samajh nahin aaya ke ye gaane bante kaise hain mujhse. God promise yaar, Uparwaale ki den hai. Varnaa* who am I, *main kaun hoon? Meri aukaat hi kya ki main songs compose kar loon aur gaa doon. Bas, Daataa meherbaan!* (I swear by God, Shweta, to this day I haven't understood how I manage to make the songs that I do. God promise, yaar, it's a gift from the Lord above. Otherwise who am I? Who am I to compose songs, to sing them? I'm a nobody. The Great Giver is kind, that's all!)'

Shweta let him carry on with his theatrics long enough to appear genuinely impressed by his humility. Then she interjected, '*Achha sun Sikandar, tu mera show karega ke nahin?* (Okay now listen, Sikandar, will you do my show or not?) I'll get you publicity beyond your wildest dreams. But you'll need to cooperate with me, okay? No-no-no-no, hang on, hang on. Before you speak—listen to my idea before you talk about money. See, my idea is to do a big series with Pakistani singers. I mean big with a capital B. One Indian and one Pakistani artiste each time, and we will call the series "Aman Bol". I tell you, it will be *such* a hit—India, Pakistan, music, peace! Have you ever been part of anything bigger?'

Even as Sikandar frowned a little at the condescension in Shweta's voice, the idea grabbed his attention. But he pretended disinterest. Smoothing his tresses back from his forehead, he took the prayer beads off his wrist and began to work them. After he had stretched the silence to breaking point, he sighed and mumbled, '*Achha?*' Years of intoning '*Maula tere karam*' and assuming divine frenzy at exactly the right moment on stage had made him a good actor; even he was inwardly surprised by the nonchalance in his voice. Then he added, 'Which Pakistani artiste do you want to present with me?'

Shweta grinned. 'Who do you think? Hayaat Ali, of course! The best from India and the best from Pakistan. It will be lovely, I tell you. *Chal,* let's finalize everything right now. Done?'

'*Jaldi kya hai, Madam ji*, what is the hurry?' said Sikandar. '*Baat-shaat to kar lein pehle.* (Let us first discuss things a bit.) And what are the dates for this *hungama* that you've planned?'

Shweta told him, trying hard not to show her irritation.

'March? Twenty-sixth? Hmmm. I'll have to see if I'm free. Okay, let me ask Sunny.'

Sunny Suneja was Sikandar's manager, known for his ruthless negotiating skills. Shweta's composure collapsed at the mention of his name, and before Sikandar could reach for his phone, she had grabbed him by the wrist and was blurting out a protest: 'No yaar, pleeeez. Don't call that bloody bastard of a manager you have. Look, I'm not going to talk to him. And if you insist, no problem, I will work with someone else. Don't mind, but it isn't as if there's a drought of artistes. There'll be others. No issues. *Tu nahin toh koi aur sahi.* I am *not* going to talk to some fuck-all manager you've appointed to squeeze money from organizers.'

Sikandar protested, '*Sunny mera manager kum bhai zyada hai.* (Sunny is more brother than manager to me.) Sunny decides my dates and rates.'

Shweta leaned forward and slapped the table with her palm. 'See, I don't understand music, Sikandar, and I don't care. *Tu* popular *hai*, and that's why I want to work with you. But you try and act smart, and I'll do the concert with someone else. You think you're a star? You think it's just the voice that matters? I'll get that chick—whatshername?—Miss Sargam. She may have disappeared from the scene now but she was a firecracker and people love an old *pataaka* that returns with a bang. I'll find her, mummy *kasam,* and I'll arrange a male-female *jugalbandi.* Or I'll find someone else, no problem. I know how to sell a concert, Sikandar Sufi. *Mere paas paisa hai, clout hai, toh main gadhe ki maa tak ko gavaa ke dikha doongi. Waah waah karne waale bhaade pe bade saare mil jaate hain. Ab bol, kya karna hai?* (I've got the money, I've got clout, I can make the mother of a donkey sing if I have to. And it's easy enough to hire crowds and critics to make a noise. Now tell me, how do you want to do this?)'

As she ranted, Sikandar assessed the situation: he'd be treading on thin ice if he insisted on involving Sunny. But he could not let this pass. He sat up in his chair, squared his shoulders and stuck his chin out. '*Chal gavaa lena gadhe ko bhi aur gadhe ki maa ko bhi. Baja lena aman ka baaja. Khush? Hayaat Ali Pakistan se aake dikha dega ki gadhaa kaun hai aur gadhe ki maa kaun. Apne India ki naak katwaa ke tujhe khushi hoti hai, toh katwaa le. Tu bhi jaanti hai, Hayaat Ali ki takkar ka koi hai toh main hoon,* only me. *Kalle jo kanna hai.*' (All right then, good luck with your donkey and its mother. Hayaat Ali will come over from Pakistan and show the world who's the donkey and who the donkey's mother. If cutting off India's nose makes you happy, go right ahead. You know very well that if there's a match for Hayaat Ali, it is me, only me. So do as you please.)'

He made as if to get up and go, but in slow motion, and Shweta struck her forehead in somewhat dramatic admission of the fact that she had let things get out of hand.

'Okay okay sorry sorry sorry,' she said. 'I shouldn't have said that. *Chal yaar*, forgive and forget.'

Sufi made a quick mental calculation: these were tough times; producers, directors, music composers didn't care about quality any longer, and had started calling winners of reality contests to dub their songs rather than pay the one-lakh-per-song dubbing fee that he commanded. As a result he had spent the last two and a half months judging a reality show titled *Sabse Sureeli Mummy*, featuring mothers who were amateur singers. Add to that the reputation of being troublesome that he had acquired after the silly fight that Sunny had gotten into with music director Gappu Mallik's secretary, which had ended with Sunny throwing his Blackberry at the secretary, leaving the fellow bleeding from the forehead. This Aman Bol concert could well be the perfect opportunity to re-establish himself as a star.

He waited for a second or two, looking at Shweta as if

he were still a little hurt and dazed. Then he opened his eyes wide, threw his head back and shook out his hair, dropped his head forward so that his silky hair curtained his face, and whispered a prayer, but loud enough for it to filter through the rich L'Oreal colours. '*Haqq Maula!*'

Shweta kept a straight face through the little performance. She knew she had made headway.

Then the sparring began again, but calibrated carefully, and in another hour it had all been decided. No money, or very little at the most. But Sikandar Sufi would be splashed on the front page of the main newspaper, TN2T, and on the cover of the group's weekly style supplement. He would also feature prominently in TV ads for the Aman Bol series, and all creatives for the campaign would carry his picture, and it would be at least ten per cent larger than the Pakistani singer's.

'Ten per cent *kyun*? Let's make it twenty per cent larger, yaar! You are so, so much better looking,' Shweta cooed.

Sikandar touched his ears and stuck his tongue out to indicate he shouldn't be greedy, and certainly not vain.

'And do you want Shwet and Meet to design something for you?'

Sikandar knew of Shwet and Meet—they were called The Sweaty Meat Shop, their label being famous for its sexy clothes—but he pretended to be puzzled. Sufi singers were in this world but not of it, after all.

'Arre,' Shweta exclaimed, 'you don't know them? They're doing all the clothes for Shah Rukh's new film!'

Sikandar nodded as if he now understood who these people were.

'Good idea, na?'

He smiled. 'As long as the company pays,' he said.

'Pay-schmay. They will be paid with an article in TN2T. About you, about the clothes for Aman Bol and about them. *Ek patthar teen shikaar*! (One stone, three birds!)'

Sufi was humbled by the woman's cunning. He would have to be careful; he had met his match. He should let her lead, he would just follow.

Shweta lived up to her word. From billboards to full-page ads, from outdoor hoardings at Mumbai's airport and major railway stations, to banners on buses and taxis, all you could see were Sikandar and Hayaat's faces—Sikandar's just a little larger—smiling down at the city from under a typographic canopy made of the words 'Aman Bol' in English, Hindi and Urdu. Radio jockeys stirred up an appropriate amount of hysteria, urging people to get their passes at the earliest or else lose a lifetime opportunity to witness two of the subcontinent's greatest singers singing for 'aman'—peace and brotherhood. Naturally, the city was in a frenzy, and crowds formed snaking queues at various locations across the city. Shweta instructed her PR team to shoot some videos of the queues and do interviews with assorted invitation seekers.

'Don't just go for the pretty young things, okay?' she instructed her team. 'Get a good variety, some aunty types, some gymmed-out types, some rich brats and some, you know, hopeless *bechaara* types. I want a nice variety, *haan?*'

Following Shweta's orders to the last letter, the Media Mines PR team churned out a series of short videos.

One featured a young mother, in canary yellow shorts and frothy lace-top, streaked hair bunched up in a topknot secured with a blinged-out hair grip, a dot of sindoor in the parting of her hair, feet smothered in toe-rings and encased in black flip-flops with bright yellow smileys printed all over them. She held her little daughter who appeared to be about four years old and was outfitted to match her mother's attire. Mama gushed without pausing to breathe:

'What I wanna say is that I lurrrrve Sikandar Sufi too too much. Minns, I'm his biggest fan I think. And me and my baby and her Daddy, we juss have to, have to, have to get passes for this concert or I will *toh* die.'

In another video, a bunch of gymmed-out men of North-Indian origin posed for the camera in T-shirts so tight their nipples threatened to pierce through the fabric. One of them declared matter-of-factly: '*Pass to bhai le ke hi jayenge aaj, varna danga ho jayega. Girlfriend ko promise diya hai ke yeh show usey pukka dikhaoonga. Toh izzat ka sawaal hai na? Samjhe aap?* (We're not leaving until we've got a pass, brother, or there'll be a riot. I've promised my girlfriend I'll take her to this show. So it's a question of honour. Get it?)'

There were also the mandatory 'nerd' with braces and 'aunty' in a nightie telling the camera how their lives would change if they could only get out of their classroom and kitchen and attend the concert.

Videos and promos for the event in all possible formats emerged with unrelenting regularity on television, in print, on radio and social media, building up a steady hype. Shweta prepared frantically to make sure that the concert went off without a hitch, ensuring that the dozens of licences and permissions required for such an event were secured swiftly and without too many questions asked.

'Follow up on those permissions from the Traffic Police Department and Fire Brigade,' she ordered her assistant. 'You're getting them today? Good! What about the AC's [Additional Collector's] office? Listen, if he acts tough and tries to be smart, just tell me. I'll get the boss to talk to him and also request the Police Commissioner. *Ek call aur seedha ho jayega* (Just one call will set him right).'

But even with every permission in place, Shweta

knew only too well that all it would take to sabotage the event was a group of protestors staging a dharna outside the concert venue demanding that all Pakistani artistes be banned from performing in India. She had, of course, ensured personally that the leaders of all political parties were duly invited, and she'd had a word with their Personal Assistants, generously handed out VVIP passes to all of them and their entourages. But there was still no guarantee that they would not be up to some mischief on the sly. It was a drug, this publicity, everyone wanted it. Badly. In the circumstances, Shweta decided it would be best to get Hayaat to reach Mumbai just a day before the event.

'Sir, let this be a short visit,' she told her boss on the phone. 'Let the Pakistani artistes come the night before the show, do a press conference in the morning, concert in the evening and return to Pakistan the very next day. No sir, don't make them wait another day for a dinner party at your residence. The longer they stay, the more trouble we could face, but your call, sir.'

And so it was that Hayaat Ali and party were flown into Mumbai on the eve of the Aman Bol event and arrangements were made to fly them back, straight to Lahore, the very next day.

Shweta met Hayaat Ali in the penthouse suite of a seven-star hotel in the city. She brought with her an enormous bunch of flowers flown in from Bangkok, flowers so glossy and magnificent, they had an air of unreality about them.

Hayaat Ali accepted the flowers courteously, with a shallow bow. Then he handed them over to the man standing behind him, whom he introduced as Asghar Ali, his manager. '*Manager toh kya, aap bas inhein mera bhai samjho Shaveta ji* (Not my manager, think of him as my brother, Shweta ji.)'

Asghar Ali, a fair, bespectacled, bald man whose eyes darted and danced uncontrollably, bowed low as he took the flowers and laid them on the dining table.

Hayaat was a tall, well-built man with a craggy, pock-marked face and a huge undershot jaw. A wide mouth with thick lips covered large tile-shaped teeth. When he sang, the jaw seemed to amplify his voice powerfully, giving it strength and an incisive quality that had become his hallmark. It was a huge voice, but one that could also perform the most acrobatic phrases with consummate ease, and carry such fine, intense emotion that when he sang of longing for Love or God, sweet, heady pain pierced his listeners' hearts. He could pass off as a wrestler off stage but on it, his shervani, his bulk and his unusual face gave him an odd gravitas. And then his voice, uncoiling powerfully, completed the spell.

There were rumours about Hayaat's gluttony, and legend had it that he consumed five tandoori chickens for each meal—apart from the naans, pulao and mutton korma that constituted his main meal. Perhaps that was why one of the girls working in Shweta's team had giggled and declared that he had a 'very non-veggie type voice', which remark had puzzled Shweta and she had put it down to either great stupidity or great sexual desire. Shweta's only concern was that the man shouldn't run up a massive hotel bill and, more, importantly, shouldn't have a coronary and die before the concert was over. But looking at him, the latter possibility seemed unlikely. Gluttonous or not, the man appeared fit and strong, and ready to take on any challenge.

Shweta was now seated opposite Hayaat and Asghar Ali, explaining to them that security had been hired for them and would be on duty outside their suite at all times. They were not to leave the hotel unescorted and it would be best if she were consulted before they went out shopping or meeting friends. As she briefed them, the doorbell chimed several times, and on each occasion hotel staff brought in goodies for the special guest staying with them—a platter of fruits, including Alphonso mangoes; special chocolates with 'Aman Bol' hand painted on them; a welcome note from the General Manager of the hotel.

The doorbell chimed yet again for the nth time, and was followed by impatient knocking on the door. An irritated Asghar answered the door and ushered in a young man with an unmistakable resemblance to Hayaat Ali.

'Shaveta ji, this is my younger brother Ghafoor Ali. He is a very good singer too and Inshallah you will also invite him to India some day,' said Hayaat Ali.

Ghafoor offered a perfunctory salaam to Shweta and leaving them to carry on with their business, proceeded to walk around the room as if he were inspecting it, opening the refrigerator and examining the mini bar and the savouries selection. What he saw did not appear to please him, and he looked increasingly grumpy as he went about the inspection.

He finally cut into the conversation: '*Bhaijaan, aap toh* room service *se mangaa lo kuchh, yahaan kuchh bhi kaam ka nahin hai. Sab* junk food type *hai, Indiya wich lagda hai ehi poplar hai.* (Bhaijaan, I think you should order something from room service, there's nothing worthwhile here. Only junk food, all of it, maybe this is the kind of stuff that's popular in India.)'

Shweta sized him up instantly and turned to Hayaat with a smile as she said: 'Please, room service *se jo aap chaahen, ya aapke bhaisahab ko jo pasand ho, wo order kar lein, kisi bhi waqt.* (Please ask room service anytime for anything you like, or whatever your brother likes.)' Then she rose to leave. '*Chaliye, toh phir kal dopehar chaar baje* press conference *ke liye milte hain. Aur us-sey pehle agar press ke kuchh log aapko contact karein, toh please interview vagaira mat dijiyega, mera number de dijiyega.* (We'll meet in the afternoon tomorrow at four for the press conference, then. And if some people from the press contact you before that, please don't give them any interviews, give them my number.) Okay then, see you soon and have a very pleasant stay in India.' With her most charming, professional smile, Shweta swept out of the room, her long dupatta heavy with zari and sequins and tassles—she had thought it appropriate for the meeting—trailing behind her.

The night and the following morning passed uneventfully, and before Shweta knew it, it was time for the press conference. She reached an hour in advance, inspected the venue and seemed satisfied with the arrangements. She sent a message each to the managers of the two artistes and was relieved when she heard from Sikandar's manager that they were on their way. It meant that at least one of the two stars would be on time for the press conference.

But from Hayaat Ali's camp there was no word, though she had messaged twice.

Shweta glanced at her phone from time to time to check if Asghar had responded, but there was nothing. At 3.40 she decided to call Hayaat's room to check on him and was alarmed when there was no response.

'Uff,' she said to her assistant, 'these bloody stars have to be treated like babies. If you don't wake them, you never know if they'd get up on time for their own damned shows! Where the hell *is* he? We'll have a PR disaster on our hands if he's late.'

She stormed out of the hall and towards the elevator. 'Let's go up to the fellow's room. I hope they haven't gone off on a Mumbai darshan, they looked just like the kind of country bumpkins who would.'

At the door of Hayaat Ali's room, she rang the doorbell several times, waiting impatiently for a response. When there was none, she rolled her hands into fists and pretended as if she wanted to pummel the door and break it down, but decided to ring the bell again. Just then the door opened, and Asghar peeped out, a frown creasing his forehead and the pupils of his eyes darting from side to side.

'*Haan ji?*' he asked.

Shweta tapped on her watch and said, '*Chaar bajne wale hain*, sir. (It's almost four.) We tried calling you and Hayaat Ali ji to remind you that in just twenty minutes the press conference will begin, but neither of you would respond. So we got worried and decided to come up and check on you.'

The crease on Asghar Ali's forehead deepened and he clucked irritably. 'Madam, you need not to worry,' he said in English to let her know just how serious he was. Then he reverted to Urdu. 'When I have said he will be there at four, he will be there exactly at four. It is my responsibility. You needn't have taken the trouble to come all the way up here.'

Shweta controlled her anger and said, 'I know, I know. Sorry for having disturbed you. We're going back now and I will send someone to escort you down at five to four.'

She turned and left as Asghar Ali shut the door on her firmly.

The venue for the press conference was one of the smaller halls on the ground floor of the hotel, to which Shweta returned. She had barely reached when Sikandar Sufi made an appearance, flanked by his personal security team of four muscular men in black. Behind them came Sunny Suneja. Shweta greeted and welcomed Sikandar and escorted him into an antechamber where she would wait with both artistes till it was time to make a grand entry with them. As they settled into the plush sofas, attendants came forward to serve refreshments and beverages.

Sunny Suneja looked around and addressed Shweta provocatively: '*Madam, woh kahaan hain, aapke Pakistani mehman? Pahunche nahin abhi? Kahin visa-shisa toh manaa nahin ho gaya? Ya plane hijack ho gaya unka?* (So where are they, Madam, your Pakistani guests? Haven't they reached? They haven't been refused visas, have they? Or has their missile failed?)'

Shweta responded with a withering look, but Sunny only smiled silkily. Shweta dispatched one of her assistants to escort Hayaat Ali and Asghar Ali to the antechamber. Minutes passed. Sherbets and teas were consumed. Then Sunny leaned forward to ask Shweta again, '*Aaye nahin?* (They haven't come?)'

Shweta ignored him and asked an attendant for another cup of tea.

'*Ab chaar toh baj gaye ji, shuru karein?* (It's four now, shall we start?) There is an artiste who is already here, you should start the conference. The *late-lateef* can take their time. There's also a concert to do, no? Or has there been a change?' Sunny was beginning to enjoy this.

Shweta looked murderously at him and hissed, '*Aap chinta mat kariye Suneja ji, aur itne utaawle bhi mat baniye* (You needn't worry, Suneja ji, and there's no need to be so impatient, either).'

She would have had more to say to Suneja but she saw that her assistant was calling.

'Ma'am, ma'am, Mr Asghar Ali is asking if Sikandar ji has arrived. He's saying Hayaat Sir will come down once Sikandar ji is there.'

'Tell him that Sikandar ji has been here for over *fifteen* minutes. So it's high time he also arrived. We are moving to the venue now, okay? He should come down *immediately*.'

She hung up and turned to Sikandar, smiling. 'You have quite a reputation, yaar, my staff are telling me people have flown in from Delhi, Amritsar, even Kolkata and Chennai to listen to you. And you know, talking to Hayaat Ali I could sense that he also admires you a lot. I don't think he would have agreed to come if it had been any other artiste...But I have a feeling he's a bit nervous...'

Sunny listened with interest. Why was she suddenly babbling so much, like a wound-up toy? And what was with all the flattery? Then he understood. But he had understood too late, for just then, Hayaat Ali walked in, with Asghar and Shweta's assistant in tow. He was a full half-hour late. Sunny would have liked Sikandar to show some displeasure at being made to wait so long, but of course Shweta, cunning woman, had ensured with all her babbling that Sunny got no time to provoke Sikandar. And now as the two artists came face to face with each other, they began to play the cordiality card to utter perfection.

The flash bulbs went wild, and photographers jostled each other. Dressed elegantly in a black shervani, Hayaat Ali stood still for some seconds, before executing a dramatic aadaab to Sikandar Sufi, bowing low. Sikandar returned the salute, bending lower and exclaiming, 'A*ha* *aha! Masha Allah! Kitne haseen lag rahe hain aap Hayaat bhai!* (By the will of Allah, how handsome you look, Hayaat bhai!)'

Then, almost in choreographed movements, the two moved to embrace each other, arms outstretched, wearing textbook smiles. As they clasped each other in a bear hug, the flash bulbs went manic again, creating a fiery halo around the two men. They posed genially for the photographers before taking their seats for the press conference. Sunny and Asghar also shook hands before taking their places behind the stars. Under their watchful eyes the press conference began, with a faded TV talk-show host in chiffon and fake pearls, who had been roped in to play presenter and moderator, introducing the two artistes in lush Urdu as 'the brightest stars in music's infinite universe'.

Everything was proceeding smoothly, but some ten minutes into the press conference, Sunny began to fret. Hayaat Ali seemed to be getting more attention, with members of the press showing greater interest in asking the foreign guest questions. After another five minutes Sunny left the low platform to go and whisper something to a couple of journalists he knew. Then he returned to his position, a smug look on his face. From the other end of the room, Shweta watched him. What was the slime-ball up to, she wondered. She didn't have to wait long to find out.

One of the journalists whom Sunny had spoken to now raised his hand. He had a question for 'our esteemed guest'.

'*Janaab*,' Hayaat acknowledged the journalist. '*Poochhiye* (Please ask),' he said, and fell right into the trap Sunny had laid for him.

'Hayaat Ali sahab, it's such a privilege to have you with us,' the journalist began. 'But sir, why is it that Pakistan does not permit Indian artistes to perform on Pakistan television? India welcomes Pakistani artistes with open arms, but the same gesture is not reciprocated in your country. Why? Any thoughts?'

'Bastard Suneja,' Shweta muttered under her breath and sprang up, in commando fashion, snatched the microphone from the presenter's hand and declared, 'Thank you, thank you so so much, ladies and gentlemen. I know you all have lots of questions for both our fabulous artistes, but they need to get ready for their concert. So please forgive me. I hope you will join us at the concert venue after the tea and refreshments that have been arranged for you. Please do come, because Aman Bol will make history. Thank you once again.'

A gaggle of bouncers descended on the artistes and swept them out of the room as photographers continued to click pictures, shouting '*Iss taraf*...*idhar, idhar sir*...Look here, this way...Sir, sir, sir!' In the brief halt outside the hotel entrance, some journalists and hotel staff managed to take selfies with Sikandar and Hayaat before they were bundled into Jaguars and sent off to the concert venue with security personnel and a police escort.

Shweta followed in another car, relieved that she was able to hold controversy at bay despite that wily Suneja—whose blood, she promised herself, she would pour into crystal goblets and drink at a time of her choosing. But for now, she braced herself for the concert.

At the venue, there were a hundred things to deal with, and time flew past. Then Sikandar was on stage, having been introduced by a Bollywood actor new and needy enough to accept possible publicity in lieu of payment.

Sikandar sang with the mix of intensity and narcissism that had made him so popular. In the wings, Hayaat Ali sat with his musicians, listening closely and uttering '*waah waah*' now and again. Soon it was his turn to take the stage, and he did so to thunderous applause from the audience that had crammed into every inch of the auditorium. They were all there—the politicians, the film stars, the veteran and new musicians, the rich and powerful, all in designer finery. Hayaat Ali sang with flamboyance and elan, ending with the song that first made him a household name in India—the traditional Punjabi Chhalla that he had sung with a neat drum and bass line. And then, as planned with

Shweta, came the *piece de resistance* of the evening. Hayaat invited his 'brother from India'—'Janaab Sikandar Sufi, *jinhin hum dil-o-jaan se chaahte hain* (whom I love with all my heart and more than my life)', on stage to sing one, just one piece with him. *Khawaateen-o-hazraat* (Ladies and gentlemen), *yeh pehle kabhi nahin hua, aur mere khayaal se Aman Bol ke alaavaa ye mumkin bhi nahin hota, ke hum dono bhai awaaz se awaaz milaakar aapki khidmat karte. Toh leejiye sahibaan...*(It has never happened before, and without Aman Bol it would indeed have been impossible that we brothers should bring our voices together in your service. So here's our offering...)'

After yet another elaborate exchange of salaams and embraces, Sikandar and Hayaat settled down to the never-before duet that was to be splashed on the front page of TN2T the next morning. Even competing newspapers would find it impossible to keep the event entirely off their front pages.

A hush fell on the audience as the two voices made an exquisite start with the *alaap*, singing almost as one—rising slowly, sinuously, circuitously, together building a radiant spread of lush *swaras*. Shweta heaved a sigh of relief. This was what she had wanted. Not so much the voices in such perfect harmony, but this media opportunity, the feeding frenzy it would cause tomorrow morning. And who had made it possible? She, Shweta Bansal. They had laughed at her in college for her accent and her clothes; they laughed at her still. They wouldn't be laughing now.

But something was changing on stage—slowly, but surely. Hayaat seemed to be gradually taking over the concert. He appeared to have cleverly steered the tapestry of notes in a direction that suited his powerful voice more, and now he was intruding every time Sikandar tried to improvise and regain control of the performance. It was almost as if Hayaat had decided that he would drown out Sikandar. Shweta frowned.

In the wings, Sunny began to fidget. And then Sikandar turned to give him a meaningful look. Sunny understood. He had permission to do whatever it took to fix things; they had discussed it only the previous evening. From her vantage point in the sound box, Shweta saw Sunny walking purposefully towards the sound console. What the hell was he doing on stage? She took her walkie-talkie and asked, 'Who gave that man permission to get on the stage?'

'Madam, he has an all-access pass,' her assistant replied.

Sunny was at the console now, talking to the engineer, and Shweta saw what he was going to do. He was going to ruin it all. How could she have underestimated the man? She had been a fool. She was certain he had bribed the sound engineer before the concert, or threatened him, blackmailed him, the rat was capable of anything.

She kicked off her stilettoes and began to run.

She heard hisses and screeches and a terrible metallic whistle pierce and tear Hayaat Ali's deep, gravelly voice to shreds. There was a split-second lull, but then a high note that Hayaat sang in anger and defiance rose to ear-splitting levels. As she ran, Shweta saw the mayor covering his ears; she heard a child howling in absolute terror; she saw the diva of the last three decades smiling a syrupy smile of satisfaction as the concert began to collapse.

Now Hayaat Ali's brother Ghafoor, who had been sitting behind Hayaat to give him company if needed, and perhaps get himself noticed too, got up and ran towards the sound console. '*Yeh kya ho rahaa hai biraadar?* (What's going on, brother?)' he confronted the sound engineer, who shrugged and pointed at Sunny.

Ghafoor turned to Sunny in a rage. Sunny smirked and gave him the finger. Ghafoor exploded. His lapel mike picked up what he was saying and what he was saying is unprintable. Suffice it to say that in the most musical Punjabi he was casting multiple and varied aspersions on the parentage and habits of the Suneja family. Sunny Suneja was replying in kind.

On stage, Sikandar and Hayaat were shocked into making an attempt to retrieve the situation—neither had bargained for this level of escalation. They sang in supreme harmony for a minute, and then gave up. It was no use. Ghafoor's and Sunny's exchange provoked them, too. They began interrupting each other, each wanting only to upstage the other, cutting in on riffs and trying to elbow the other man vocally out of the way.

Then Shweta Bansal reached the stage, a little out of breath, and without hesitating, picked up a mike and said, 'Thank you, *shukriya, dhanyawaad,* for a lovely evening, for some lovely music. I know we could have gone on all night but we have some constraints. Goodnight, *shubh raatri, shab-ba-khair.*'

In just a few minutes, the concert was over, and the artistes were making their way through the audience into their hired Jaguars. Sikandar got into his and Sunny got in after him. As the sleek, beautiful car slid through the streets of the sleepless city, Sikandar said, '*Zara zyada ho gaya, yaar Sunny.* (It got a little out of hand, Sunny.)' He was quiet for a bit, looking out of the window, then he sighed, '*Aman-shaman...Saaddi zindgi vich te neyi.* (Peace-veace...Not in our lifetime.)'

Foreign Returned

For decades Asavari Apte, Hindustani classical vocalist and teacher from Pune, had longed to bag a 'foreign' tour. She knew she could do it, she was the right person to be an ambassador of India's ancient musical heritage and its evolved system of classical music; she lived it, she *was* it. She just needed a chance to show her mettle, and though the years seemed to be passing swiftly and the furthest they took her from Pune was Delhi and Kolkata, Lucknow and Udaipur, she still hoped that she would soon be jet-setting across the globe, her tanpura tucked under her arm, her saris just the right colour, her talent obvious to anyone who knew anything about classical music.

And finally it was here, her big chance. She was in Philadelphia, USA, in the sprawling home of the Mohite couple and their eight-year-old daughter Sulabha. The Mohites were crazy about Hindustani classical music and frequently offered to host visiting Indian artistes, especially if they came from their native Maharashtra. When they heard that Asavari would be touring America, they immediately contacted fellow Maharashtrian and President of the Indian Music Society of Philadelphia (IMSP), Shrirang Ambekar, and offered to host Asavari for the length of her stay in the city. Ambekar accepted their offer eagerly because it meant that the organization could save a little money, and also because Minal and Manjul Mohite were reputed to be very hospitable. He knew they could be relied upon to take care of Asavari and do everything possible to make her stay comfortable. Frankly, he was hugely relieved as well. Visiting Indian musicians could be quite a pain in the neck, often demanding constant attention and hand-holding. It would be a huge responsibility off his hands to have the Mohites take care of the Apte lady.

So here she was with the Mohites, seated on the rug in their living room, with their daughter Sulabha singing Raag Bhupali to her. The little girl was tuneful and had been taught well by her mother, but as could be expected of any Indian child born and brought up in the United States, her American accent often stood out rather strongly in her Bhupali. '*Itno joban purrr maan na curriye*' she sang earnestly, accompanied by a tanpura and tabla generated from an app on her Mum's phone.

The phone was connected to a bluetooth speaker which, sadly, amplified the tanpura and tabla sounds in a rather unflattering way. *Bong bing binga, bong bing pinga, bong bing pinga, bong bing binga* went the tabla mechanically, the sound distorted on being amplified. And the tanpuras hissed sibilantly like manic mosquitos swarming around the little singer.

Sulabha was singing sargams now, and every time she sang Pancham or Pa, she pronounced it as Pha—Ga Pha Pha, Ga Pha Pha, Ga Pha Da Pha Ga Rrrrray Sa. Dhaivat became Da instead of Dha and soon Asavari felt an almost irrepressible urge to giggle. But she willed herself to nod appreciatively, offering the little singer an occasional encouraging '*waah*'. The little girl continued for another ten minutes, singing each line and every variation twice. Jet-lagged, Asavari came close to dozing off in between, and struggled to stifle persistent yawns but finally, Sulabha ended with a *tihai*. As she finished, she looked expectantly at her mother, who in turn looked hopefully at Asavari for encouragement. Asavari applauded and praised the child's singing, saying, '*Chhaan! Khupach chhaan.* (Really very good.)'

'Honestly, tai? Please be frank, do you think she shows any promise?' Minal Mohite asked.

'Of course! Means…she is very, very promising and talented,' replied Asavari in a pronounced Marathi accent, 'and she will improve as she learns and does *riyaaz*. Definitely, she will improve.'

Mother and daughter exchanged happy smiles which Mum followed up with a request. 'Do you think you might teach her something? A little *bandish*? Or a *bhajan*? Or whatever you think appropriate? It will be such an honour for her, she will remember it all her life.'

'Maybe tomorrow? Right now I am still a little tired, you know?' said Asavari rather hesitantly. 'Maybe jate-lag or something.'

'No, no problem,' said Minal, making no effort to hide her disappointment. Asavari felt a twinge of guilt and wondered if she should have held herself together for a little longer to teach little Sulabha a small composition, but the matter was decided in a trice by the little girl herself.

'Mom,' she chirped excitedly, 'I've been good, haven't I? Now can I go watch TV? Pleeeeze?' Delighted at receiving permission from her mother, she skipped and hopped up the stairs with Minal warning her that she would have to be ready to go to bed in half an hour.

Asavari wished her hostess good night and made her way to the basement where a mattress and bedding had been laid out for her on the carpeted floor. She would have preferred a bed, she would have preferred a room with a view, a window, but the Mohites had been so polite that she felt she shouldn't complain. Perhaps they really had no bed to spare; life in the West, she had heard, was expensive business. Or maybe they had heard that she, Asavari, was a simple person who lived frugally, and had assumed that she preferred to sleep on the floor. Well, she would let them think that; a reputation for austerity was an asset in her chosen field.

But now, as she lay down, she realized that the mattress was horribly lumpy. It would have been very uncomfortable and kept her awake all night in usual circumstances. But she was so tired that she drifted into a deep sleep almost the moment her head hit the pillow.

She woke up the next morning a little disoriented. It took a while for it to register that she was not in her flat in Pune but in the basement of a house in America. Now she heard the great Marathi singer Sudhir Phadke's beautiful voice wafting from the room above, singing a popular song from his 'Geet Ramayan': '*Swaye Shri Ram Prabhu aikati, Kush-Lav Ramayan gaati.*' As she lay in bed, she started singing along with the track to test her voice, relieved at hearing something so familiar and well-loved. Her voice sounded a little hoarse and she cleared her throat a couple of times, then she got up, folded the bedding neatly and prepared to dress and get ready.

The Mohite family was up and about when she walked in on them in the large kitchen and dining area. Minal was bustling about, finishing chores as the family listened to music and had breakfast. They greeted her warmly and Minal announced that she and her husband had taken leave from work to spend time with her and perhaps take her into the city to shop or meet people she might know. Asavari turned down the idea, saying, 'Oh no no no, please don't bother. I'm not at all interested in shopping, and I don't know anyone here. As you know, this is my first trip to USA, or shall I say first foreign trip only, and I have no friends here whom I can visit.'

The Mohite couple were slightly irritated by her response but made a quick recovery. 'Okay, but what about some sightseeing? There are some lovely walking tours and food tours that you might enjoy. Or museums? No?' asked Minal cheerfully.

There was a brief spark of interest in Asavari's eyes at this, but then she said, hesitantly, 'They must be ticketed, no?'

'Yes, I think the tickets are around thirty to forty dollars.'

'Per person?' Asavari asked.

Behind her, Manjul rolled his eyes. Minal shot him a stare and said, 'Yes, tai, per person.'

'Forty dollars must be about 2500 rupees, no? *Nako re baba*. Too expensive. I have come here for music and let me do my music properly and go back to where I belong.

That will be more than enough for me. You please don't bother about all this sightseeing and shopping and all that.'

The Mohites were not surprised. Most Indian artistes they hosted showed scant interest in sight-seeing or catching a show or movie, unless of course someone else paid for them. Eager to show Asavari a good time under their watch, Minal made another valiant attempt to entice her out of the house. Would she like to go out for a meal and try some of the specialty restaurants in the city?

Asavari declined again, and this time firmly: 'Actually, I like Indian food best. Even in Pune my students often ask me to come out for burger, pizza and all. But I always tell them I like my *varan-bhaat* best. No need to take me to some fancy restaurant and waste money unnecessarily. Simple daal-bhaat will do.'

The Mohites were left with no option but to stay home with her. But little Sulabha who was eager and ready for an outing hurled herself at her mother and asked petulantly, 'Mom, why aren't we going out? You *promised* we would.'

Asavari urged the couple to go ahead without her instead of disappointing Sulabha by abandoning their plans. The couple looked at each other awkwardly, unable to decide if they should take up Asavari's suggestion, but eventually decided to drive to a beautiful lake nearby.

'There's a lot of food in the refrigerator,' instructed Minal before she left. 'You just need to take it out and warm it in the microwave. Would you be fine doing that? Do you want me to show you how?'

This time it was Asavari who was a little irritated, and she made no effort to conceal it. 'I do know how to use a microwave. You please don't worry, I will be fine, just fine.'

Then she felt she had been rude, so she went to the door with the family when they left. She smiled and waved as they drove off, turned, shut the door and moved to the basement, heaving a sigh of relief at having some time to herself. Lying back on the lumpy makeshift bed she gazed up at the ceiling as she thought about how she had finally managed to get here.

She smiled wryly as she remembered her futile efforts to secure a tour through the Indian Arts Association for Cultural Exchange (IAACE), which regularly sent Indian artistes overseas on performing and teaching assignments. But to even be considered for an overseas tour through the IAACE, one had to overcome the seemingly insurmountable challenge of being empanelled with them. She had applied several years ago for empanelment, submitting all the documentation required for the process with the greatest sincerity. But a decade later, the application was still pending and every attempt she made to get an update had been unsuccessful. Her emails went unanswered, her letters were ignored, and she had lost count of how many minutes she had spent listening to the hollow ringing of the landline, as if resounding in a deserted office. When she did get someone on the line, it was never the Programme Officer in charge of empanelment. He/she was never on his/her seat. Or he/she was on tour. Or he/she was on leave. He/she was always somewhere else; in a place where Asavari could not talk to him/her.

Asavari finally gave up. After all, there was no guarantee that even after empanelment she would be offered an overseas tour.

And she had heard recently from reliable sources that there had been a change of guard at the IAACE office, and currently the organization seemed to show a marked preference for artistes from West Bengal. Apparently, certain senior artistes in the selection committee for empanelment of artistes were Bengalis and they, with the active encouragement of certain IAACE senior officials, also Bengalis, had taken it upon themselves to show the world that West Bengal was the fountainhead of all Indian art.

'Ah well,' Asavari thought to herself, 'let West Bengal have its day.' Because only a few years back, it had been the 'Tam-Brahm'—Tamilian Brahmin—lobby that held sway over IAACE. And during that period Bharatanatyam dancers from every nook and corner of Tamil Nadu had a field day touring overseas on IAACE funding. If whispers among disgruntled Kathak dancers were to be believed, the Bharatanatyam artistes were permitted to take along their entire families as members of their ensembles. And of course they were reimbursed for any item they listed as a professional expense, including nail varnish, *aalta*—the red dye used by dancers to decorate their hands and feet—hairspray, makeup kits and even dark glasses.

To be fair, the Maharashtrian lobby too had had its heyday when Union Minister Narendra Rao Naaktode held the Information and Broadcasting portfolio and was a member of the IAACE advisory. But that had been some twenty years ago.

But the main reason why Asavari had given up on her application for empanelment was the experience another vocalist, also from Pune, had had some years ago. Asavari had heard of it from the lady herself. This lady, Sharada, had been sent to Russia on tour by IAACE, and was made to sing *alaaps* for a fashion show in St. Petersburg where a designer was exhibiting lingerie and leather boots. Fearing that she would be blacklisted if she protested or refused to comply, Sharada had no option but to sing *alaaps* in Jaijaiwanti and Maru Bihag as terrifyingly tall, unsmiling models dressed in knee-length leather boots and lace underwear sashayed past her, occasionally striking a leather whip against their boots.

It was all for the best, then, Asavari told herself, that she hadn't managed to get empanelled with IAACE.

And yet, here she was in the USA, on tour finally. It was all thanks to Upendra Oak, a young and talented Pune-based tabla player who was steadily gaining popularity among vocalists in India, both for his skilled and sensitive accompaniment and, in equal measure, for his ability to organize and manage overseas concert tours for the vocalists he accompanied.

Asavari knew absolutely nothing about his skills as an impresario and tour manager when she first met him. Just about a year ago he was sent to her for *riyaaz* by his guru, Pandit Gangadhar Godbole, a leading tabla guru with dozens of awards and accolades to his credit, like the Maharashtra Mahima and Laya Saadhak awards. 'He is a good fellow and has a flair for accompanying vocal music,' Pandit Godbole had explained to Asavari. 'I think you will enjoy his accompaniment and he too will benefit and learn from the experience. And if he acts smart, just give me a call and I will pull him up.'

Indeed, Upendra was all that his guru had promised he would be and gave Asavari no cause whatsoever for complaint. Everything went well for about a year, but then suddenly Asavari noticed a pronounced swagger in his manner. She also noted that the fulsome praise and deep respect with which he always spoke about his guru seemed to have evaporated and now he hardly mentioned Pandit Godbole. Not setting too much store by this obvious sign of friction between guru and disciple, Asavari decided not to coax any information from Upendra on the subject. After all, the relationship between guru and *shishya* often soured. Just as children fought with their parents from time to time, *shishyas* sometimes had problems with their gurus. But then they usually found a way through. It would all be fine soon enough, she reassured herself.

Things did not improve, and Asavari found out the truth far sooner than she had thought she would. One day Upendra reached her place for *riyaaz* a good half hour before the scheduled time and asked if she could spare time for a brief chat. They settled down in the living room, across each other, and he began: 'Tai, I wanted to ask if you would be interested in doing a USA tour with me this year.'

Asavari stared at him, dumbstruck, wondering if she was hallucinating. This young chit of a fellow! How could he even think of a USA tour? And how could he invite her? Perhaps his guru was thinking of organizing a tour with her, and the ambitious young lad was trying to hijack his guru's plans? Uncertain of how she should respond, she pretended not to have heard and leaned forward to ask, '*Kai re*, what did you say? I'm sorry but I didn't hear properly.'

'Tai, I asked if you would consider doing a US tour with me later this year.'

'*Arre pann* who is inviting me to the US, *baal?* I'm happy to perform with you anywhere, in India, China or USA. But no one is inviting me to USA,' she giggled self-consciously. 'I was just telling my students the other evening that soon I will be the only vocalist in Pune to never have performed in America, or for that matter anywhere outside India, not even in Nepal or Bangladesh!'

'That's where I come in, Tai. I have made many contacts in USA who arrange P3 visas for me and I have been organizing tours with artistes for the past year or so on a professional basis. But of course these were all young, new artistes. Now that all my arrangements are properly worked out, I would like to organize a tour with an *apratim* artiste like you. I know that music lovers in the US are keen to hear you live, and I will be able to line up quite a few concerts for you.'

For decades Asavari had dreamt of this moment, and now, when she had all but given up hope, this young fellow was saying he could make it happen, just like that, as if it was like taking the train to Mumbai! Astounded and incredulous, she decided to tread cautiously and started by asking Upendra what his guru thought of the idea.

Her question immediately triggered off a rapid and long-winded explanation: 'Actually, tai, I'm no longer going to Guru ji for *taaleem*. You see, last year he was away in USA for two tours, each three months long. That meant he was away for half the year, and before he left he was busy with all the visa-shiza, preparations for the tours, so his students got no time or attention from him.'

He stopped, thought for a moment and then continued, 'Tai, I'm no longer taking *taaleem* from Guruji. You see, on the rare occasions that he called me for training, I was made to sit in a group class with ten other students and not given any individual attention. I don't mind learning in a group, but this was a group of beginners that I was made to join. And then it became very evident that he seemed to favour another *shaagird*, a guy who cannot play to save his life, but whose father is very close to the Chief Minister's family and many other powerful politicians. Earlier, whenever there were any opportunities to perform or accompany Guru ji anywhere, he always selected me. But now I was left behind and this chap, Surve, would be the only one he ever took along. Meanwhile I would be asked to coach the group in Guru ji's absence, so I was left doing *dha tete, dha tete* with the class while Surve posed as his pet disciple at all events. I was also expected to answer all of Guru ji's letters, emails, all his correspondence. In short, I became not just his *shaagird* but also his secretary. Tai, I promise I was happy to serve him as long as I was treated fairly. But the problem is that Guru ji can no longer see beyond Surve, and there is a reason for that. Guru ji is planning to start a big tabla school in Pune and wants to get land at subsidized rates from the government. For that, Surve will be more helpful than any other *shaagird*. So Surve gets Guru ji's attention while we just hang around like jokers. Tai, please don't think I'm an ingrate. You know how devoted I was to Guru ji. But now I feel I need to look out for myself. And since I was handling all Guru ji's email correspondence with his US partners, I finally asked them if they would work with me independently and they agreed. That is my story, tai, and it's absolutely true.'

Asavari listened in complete shock to the entire story and thought, 'Baba! Imagine pulling the rug from under your guru's feet. I don't think I could have done something so bold ever.'

But to Upendra she spoke in the tone of an elder offering sound advice to a juvenile. '*Baal*, have you thought about this carefully and tried to patch things up with your guru? You know as well as I do that in our field a guru's blessings are essential. Why part ways with him in such an ugly manner?'

'Yes, tai,' interrupted Upendra, 'you are right. I too would have liked to leave on cordial terms. But as of now I'm forbidden from ever entering his home or even announcing anywhere that I'm his disciple. Guru ji even summoned my father and told him to ensure that I never set foot in his house or even his locality, or else his disciples would break my arms in so many pieces that I would never again be able to use them for anything, leave alone play the tabla. He abused me in such foul language, even though my mother was present, that my parents were deeply troubled and decided to approach the police. I tried my best to talk them out of it but naturally they were concerned about my safety and went ahead and filed a complaint against Guru ji. Now there is no possibility of ever mending bridges with him, tai. It's over. Finished. For good.'

Asavari could not help putting a hand over her mouth in horror. Imagine threatening a disciple with such violence! Even if the fault lay with Upendra, surely Godbole should have been mindful of his exalted status as guru and tempered his response? What was the world coming to! She wondered for a moment if Godbole might call her and threaten her with dire consequences too if she collaborated with Upendra.

But it did not take long for Upendra to convince Asavari that she would be in good hands with him, and that her US tour would be even better than any that his guru could have organized for her. Trying hard to contain her excitement, she unloaded a barrage of questions upon Upendra. What about the harmonium accompaniment, she asked. Would they take someone from Pune? 'No, tai,' Upendra explained patiently. 'To keep costs down we will book a harmonium player from the US. There are many good musicians there and I will send you a list to select from. Taking someone from India on your very first tour won't be possible.'

Although Asavari studiously avoided bringing up the matter of performance fees, Upendra took the bull by the horns and told her, 'Tai, I would like to explain everything about the money and fee too, but since you've called me for *riyaaz* now and I can see that your students are already at the gate, I can come some other time and explain everything or stay back after the *taaleem* and then explain things to you.'

Asavari replied nonchalantly, 'Whatever is more convenient for you, because as you know, I am in no hurry.'

Later that evening, as Upendra explained the math to Asavari, he shattered several myths about 'foreign tours' that she had harboured for years.

'Let me explain, tai,' he began in a no-nonsense tone. 'In terms of money, I can't tell you how much money you or I can make on such a tour. In fact, no promoter, not even Guru ji, can tell you that. Because that's the way it is. I will start by trying to get at least three or four confirmed formal concerts for you in USA and Canada, and once I'm able to secure these, I will try and contact other groups and organizations as well. If we are lucky, we might get ten to fifteen house concerts too. But please remember that house concerts are on voluntary donation basis, so we won't really know how much money to expect from those concerts. My experience tells me that it would be reasonable to expect a thousand to thousand five hundred dollars from each house concert. And about three to four thousand dollars from the bigger concerts, if we are lucky. But the good thing is that the concerts take place on weekends as most of the organizers and hosts work during the week and can't take time off to arrange concerts. But during the week, we can arrange for you to teach and that will bring some extra income for you if you are open to the idea. Okay? Is that clear? Do you have any questions?'

Asavari shook her head and Upendra continued, 'So now let me explain that from the money that comes in from concerts and teaching assignments, we need to pay for visa fees, flight tickets, plus there will be some expenses and processing fee to be given to the organization that will file the visa petitions for us. And for the bigger concerts, the organizations might provide hotel accommodation for a day or two, but for the rest of the trip we need to find music lovers, friends, relatives in the US who will be willing to host us at their homes. Do you have any family, students—anyone you know in the US? No? Not a single person? Really? Oh. Anyway, it shouldn't be tough to find hosts, because *aaple* Maharashtrians are there, many of them, and they are always welcoming us artistes from Maharashtra. *Khara mhanje*, in some ways it turns out to be far more economical if you stay with Indian families. You don't have to spend on food, laundry, so many other things. But of course, you have to eat as per their taste and accept whatever arrangements they make for you.'

Upendra continued to talk animatedly, unstoppably, providing the smallest details, stressing important points like the commission he would charge for his own role...

As she lay on her makeshift bed in the Mohites' basement in Philadelphia for a nap, Asavari now smiled to herself as she recalled the entire drama of Upendra inviting her for a US tour and the flurry of activity that followed. *Aai ga*! How much *barh-barh* this Upendra was capable of!

Just then she heard the front door open and the Mohites return.

'Yoohooo, we're home,' yodelled Sulabha. Asavari tidied up and walked up the stairs to meet them. She stopped short when she saw that there were two more Indian couples with the Mohites and smiled uncertainly as they rushed to touch her feet. Minal introduced them as Mira and Hari, Kuhu and Soumik.

'Tai, they are true music lovers and always help out

and volunteer at all our classical music concerts. But they're also deeply spiritual and do a lot of *sadhana*, and they really want to invite you to an event that their spiritual leader is organizing. Go on, ask her yourselves,' she urged the smiling visitors.

'Ma,' began Soumik, in a deep voice, with folded hands and respectfully lowered eyes, 'as Minal just told you, we are learning meditation and *bhakti* from our guru, an American gentleman who is also a musician and very spiritual. He has many followers here. In fact, his disciples from different states gather here in Philadelphia for Holi every year.'

Soumik's wife Kuhu interjected breathlessly: 'Actually, our Holi celebrations are becoming bigger and bigger and last year we had about twenty-five thousand people for the Utsav!'

Soumik waited for his wife to finish and resumed with a reverent 'Jai Gurudeb', which he uttered with his hands outstretched and eyes turned heavenwards. 'So Ma, what we have been doing to attract young people, and not only young Indians but people from across the world, is to get DJs from our group to play music at the Utsav. This year we want to have a small contest of DJs to select the three best for the Utsav, and Ma, we would be most grateful if you could be a judge for the contest next weekend. I believe you may be free on that weekend?'

Asavari looked a little bewildered and said hesitantly, 'You see, I am not knowing too much about this DJ and all. My music is only classical and I am not familiar with all this.'

'Oh no no Ma,' protested Soumik, 'these DJs are all followers of Gurudeb, so when they play it's all *shlokas* and mantras and, you know, devotional poetries.'

Mira had been quiet all along, but she now chimed in: 'Why don't we show Mata ji a video of last year's Utsav? She will understand immediately.'

'That's such a great idea!' exclaimed Kuhu and soon they were all in the family room with Asavari ensconced in a deep armchair, while Hari set things up on the enormous smart TV. With great pride, he selected a video on YouTube and played it. As it played, the foursome, Mira, Hari, Kuhu and Soumik, swayed from side to side, moving to the music, and after a few minutes, began to jump up and down in ecstasy as the tempo increased. Minal and Manjul were a trifle subdued, but smiling and clapping along occasionally. Asavari, on the other hand, cowered in the armchair, eyes wide open at what she was witnessing. These were very strange people! Alarmed by their devotional frenzy, she turned to the TV screen.

In the massive grounds of an opulent marble temple complex were thousands of people, gathered for what seemed to be a rock concert. The crowd, bobbing and jumping and head banging, was led by a group of nine musicians on stage—four men and five women. None of them seemed to be from India, though the women were in Indian clothes. Two were in full Bharatanatyam regalia, including *ghungroos* on their feet. The three other women were in *lehngas* and colourful T-shirts with contrasting dupattas tied across their bodies. All five had stick-on bindis pasted in elaborate patterns across their foreheads. The men wore jeans and T-shirts, but all of them had a *shikha,* the tuft of hair worn long at the back of the head by Brahmins and priests. When they jumped as they performed, the *shikhas* also bobbed up and down. One of the women played a harmonium, the men worked turntables, and the Bharatanatyam dancers positioned themselves on either side of the stage to lead people through dance moves that should have been graceful but were plain ridiculous. A colourful banner announced that this was Holi with DJ KK (Kirtan Klan).

DJ KK chanted into the mike—

> Say Raddey Raddey baybee, and you will
> get Nirrvanner
> Say Krishna Krishna baybee, you're sure to
> find Ananndder

The Bharatanatyam dancers now had their hands up in the air and were soon doing a typical Bhangra move, which the crowd followed ecstatically. After the Bhangra, they switched to hip-hop moves like the Egyptian tutt.

At regular intervals, bursts of colour and confetti were cannoned into the air, with the crowds cheering and erupting in further jubilation.

Everyone in the room seemed to be enjoying the spectacle. But Asavari decided it was time she indicated that she could not, simply could not accept their invitation. She gestured, indicating that the volume be turned down or the video stopped, and then proceeded to say, 'You see, in our Maharashtra also I have seen and heard high-energy *kirtan* and *gondhal* and all, but that is traditional and I am somewhat familiar with it. Now this music and this style, I do not know, and I do not even understand the American accent in the lyrics. So I will not be able to judge this contest, *haan*? Sorry, don't mind, okay?'

'Awwww please don't say no,' pleaded Kuhu. 'It would be such an honour for us to have you at the contest.'

But Asavari held fast and announced in a prim voice, 'Please understand, baba, what I have said to you. When I don't know anything about this DJ and all, how I can judge the competition?'

Disappointed, the two couples took their leave after they realized that Asavari would not be coaxed into accepting their invitation. Soumik made one last attempt as they left: 'Ma, if you do change your mind, let us know even at the last minute.'

'No,' came the curt and prompt response, 'I won't change my mind.'

Mira grimaced, showing more displeasure than disappointment, but joined the gang in touching Asavari's feet before they left.

Two weeks passed swiftly as Asavari and Upendra settled into the tour. The Mohites had not invited Upendra to stay with them so he was hosted by another Maharashtrian family somewhere in a distant part of town. It meant that Asavari saw him only during concerts—of which there had been two, one in Philly and the other in New Jersey—and a private performance for a family of three stern-looking Bengali ladies. The private performance had been a stiff affair, but the concerts had been well received, though the one in New Jersey was not very well attended. And now they had a house concert in Phoenixville coming up next.

So far, Asavari felt, the tour had been fairly good, despite her having to live with complete strangers in a completely unfamiliar environment, in a basement room that sometimes made her feel claustrophobic. But the Mohites were good to Asavari and she was grateful for their kindness and hospitality. And at the last concert a few Americans had sat in the front row listening to her in rapt attention. Perhaps it was a sign of bigger things to come. She had been in the shadows too long.

It was in Phoenixville that the tour slowly started to curdle.

Upendra had told Asavari very categorically that the harmonium accompanists for her concerts would have to be from the US, and she had left the task of selecting and engaging them to Upendra. She did not know much about their musicianship but trusted Upendra to make a wise choice. He had not disappointed her so far and the young software engineer Sunil Bhatt, who had accompanied her for two concerts, was both competent and professional. She presumed he would be present for the house concert too. But when she reached Phoenixville and met Upendra at the venue, he informed her that Bhatt was not available for the concert, and so he had 'booked someone new'.

'It will be fine, don't worry,' he assured her, but he would not meet her eye, causing alarm bells to go off in her head. Before she could question him further, a young woman accompanied by a turbaned Sikh came and stood before her. Both touched her feet respectfully, the young lady muttering a soft '*Pairi pauna ji*'. Asavari smiled back at the couple and noted the girl's attire. She was dressed in a powder-pink lace sari with a matching, sequinned backless blouse, and wore dozens of *choodas*, the red-and-white bangles favoured by young Punjabi brides, all the way up to her elbows. There were silver rings on all her fingers, and her unusually long nails were painted in shiny red and white. As Asavari prepared to tune up, the young lady announced: 'I'm Manpreet, and I'm gonna play tanpura with you.'

Asavari looked askance at Upendra, but he appeared engrossed in taking the tablas out of his bag.

'Where would you like me to sit?' Manpreet asked.

Asavari pointed to a spot a little behind her on the left and took up the tanpura placed in front of her to tune it. It was then that she realized that the harmonium accompanist was yet to arrive. Upendra shrugged when she asked him. 'He should be here any minute,' he said.

Asavari started tuning with the iTanpura app on her phone for reference, and once she was satisfied, she handed over one tanpura to Manpreet, and began playing the other one herself. As she listened intently to the tanpuras to check if the tuning was accurate, she began to hear a strange, discordant scraping sound. A deep frown emerged on her forehead as she listened more closely to the jangle interspersed with a metallic *tssssik-tssssik*, as if someone was scraping two pieces of metal against each other. She could not find anything wrong with the tuning of the tanpura she was playing so she leaned towards the tanpura Manpreet was playing, and discovered to her horror that the maddening sound came from Manpreet's painted talons scratching the strings of the tanpura. How could she possibly sing with this terrible sound? She turned towards Upendra and addressed him agitatedly in Marathi.

'Upendra, my head will burst if I have to hear this

through the concert. I will go mad. Please do something. I don't mind singing with just one tanpura, but I can't bear this.'

'Okay, okay,' said Upendra in a placatory tone as he walked off to work out a strategy with the host.

He returned in a few minutes with the host in tow, who walked over to Manpreet, crouched in front of her and started explaining something in a whisper. In the meantime, Upendra studiously started tuning his tablas. Suddenly, Manpreet put the tanpura down and flounced off to her escort, and both left the room in a huff, with the host hurrying after them. Upendra leaned towards Asavari and explained conspiratorially in Marathi that he had requested the host to tell Manpreet that the tanpura she was playing had not been maintained properly and therefore could not be played today.

But there was more in store for Asavari that evening. Just when she had said a small prayer and thanked Upendra for handling the situation so well, along came another shock. This time it was in the form of a young man, seemingly of Indian origin, dressed in shabby track pants and a black T-shirt with the slogan LET THEM EAT SHIT printed on it, which Asavari found outrageous. Would she be singing for people like this now? Nothing about him looked right to her. His left arm was tattooed from the wrist all the way up to the top of his arm. The right side of his neck was also covered in tattoos. He wore his hair long, and his oily locks were held in place by a bright blue band across his forehead. His eyes seemed runny, and there was a scruffy air about him. He carried a faded canvas bag with him which he put down on the floor as he came and stood in front of Asavari and Upendra silently, making no effort to introduce himself.

Upendra looked up at him and asked, 'Vineet? Are you Vineet?'

'Yeah man,' he said gruffly, 'you Upendra?'

Upendra nodded.

'Okay, so here I am.'

He removed a small harmonium from the canvas bag and settled himself on the floor to Asavari's left.

'*Sur?*' he asked Asavari.

'*Kaaye?*' she demanded of Upendra.

'He'll play the harmonium for us,' he said, trying not to look her in the eye.

'*Sur*, lady,' the young man said.

'A. *Kaali paanch*,' she replied, trying to keep the anger out of her voice.

He winced a little and said, 'That isn't too comfortable for me. Can you change that to either G# or A#?'

Asavari glared at Upendra, who felt singed. 'I'm sorry,' he mumbled in Marathi. 'We will have to make do with whatever is available. This is a very small town and I had no alternative.'

'And I suppose I will also have to accept that *shloka* he has on his T-shirt?'

'No no, I'll try and get him to change,' said Upendra.

Vineet interjected,'So guys, have you decided whether it's going to be G# or A#?'

'A#,' Asavari snapped and proceeded to re-tune the tanpura.

Once the performance began, Asavari concentrated on the music and soon forgot any irritation Manpreet and Vineet might have caused. She did, however, take care not to look at the the latter's T-shirt, which he had refused to exchange with the colourful kurta the host had offered him for the performance. Asavari's music captivated the audience and they plied her with many requests, most of which she smilingly accepted and complied with.

Once the concert ended, she was surrounded by people, some of whom spoke to her in Marathi, others who dragged reluctant teenagers to meet her and take her blessings, and still others who wondered if she might have time to give them a class or two. She directed all of them towards Upendra, who was now ensconced behind a little table near the entrance to the room, selling her CDs for those who wished to purchase them. He was stuffing the dollars people gave him for the CDs into a leather pouch he usually carried with him. As she met people and exchanged pleasantries with them, Asavari noticed a glass fish-bowl perched on the tabla. She saw the hostess pointing in the direction of the bowl as people walked by, almost as if she was drawing their attention to it and reminding them of something. Curious, Asavari looked on. She saw people putting cash contributions into the bowl—some music lovers withdrew dollar bills from their wallets and deposited them in the fish bowl, others dug into their pockets, brought out some coins and dropped them into the bowl. Asavari felt her face flush in embarrassment as she realized what Upendra had meant when he had said payments from house concerts could not be calculated in advance as entry was on voluntary contribution. But she had not imagined *this*! Shouldn't he have mentioned that it would be like singing and begging in the streets? Feeling deeply humiliated, Asavari wished she could return to India that very minute. So this is the truth about the 'foreign' tours that everyone talks about? she asked herself. '*Baal*,' she wanted to say to Upendra, 'you should have told me the truth. Now let's go back, I don't want any more of this.'

Sadly, there was no opportunity for her to confront Upendra and question him. The Indian family hosting Upendra was waiting patiently to take him home with them, and another Indian family had been recruited to drop Asavari back to the Mohites' residence. She did manage briefly to catch Upendra's attention on their way out and to ask him if she could meet him somewhere the next day or the day after, but as he packed and loaded his tablas into the car, he announced hurriedly that he would not be available till the next weekend. When Asavari looked concerned, he explained that he had received an invitation to accompany someone in Houston and since they didn't have a concert till the next weekend, he thought he would make good use of his time. With a deep frown lining her brow, Asavari said, 'Strange, that you shouldn't tell me about this till I asked.'

'No no, tai, this was really last minute, and I would have told you but it just slipped my mind. Actually, it's this jazz group I'm playing with, so you just relax with the Mohites and I will be back soon.'

He was gone before she could even wrap her muffler around her throat properly. Troubled by the day's surprises and shocks, she sat quietly all through the ride to the Mohites' home, and was glad to be back with them finally.

Through the week, there were several moments when Asavari brooded over the problems she had encountered during the tour, but she also wondered if she was being difficult. After all, so many hundreds of musicians from India toured America every year, she told herself, and they too must have done these house concerts. She had even seen some Facebook posts of house concerts they had uploaded. If they didn't have a problem with the 'voluntary contributions' being dropped into a beggar's bowl, maybe she was just being unreasonable and snobbish. Times had changed, after all. And the harmonium player with that indecent slogan on his T-shirt? What of that? Wasn't that shameful, wasn't it insulting? But then, she reasoned with herself, even in India there had been times when she was accompanied by mediocre musicians, some of whom were sloppily dressed or lacking in manners. There was even a time when an accompanist had turned up drunk for a performance. So why get agitated about this one concert where she'd had to perform with a hippie type harmonium player? Maybe she should just let it be. But how could she? That...that T-shirt...Classical music was sacred. No, she could not pretend it was a small matter. It was very wrong, it wouldn't do. What was Upendra thinking? And finally, why wasn't she told that he would accept concerts with other artistes during *her* tour? He hadn't ever mentioned that, not once. She would definitely take that up with him. Yes, she would. Let him get back; she would demand a meeting.

Asavari waited patiently for the phone to ring on Friday, when Upendra was to return from Houston. She hadn't got herself a local SIM, so Upendra either sent her text messages or called on the Mohites' landline. As expected, the phone rang at about 7.30 in the morning and she heard Minal speaking to someone. She presumed

Minal would call out for her if it was Upendra, but when Minal continued the conversation she guessed it was someone else and drifted back into sleep. She didn't hear Minal walk down to the basement and was startled when she heard her call out and say, 'Asavari Tai, Asavari Tai, wake up, please. We need to talk. We have a situation on our hands. It seems Upendra has been arrested in Houston along with two other musicians he was playing with.'

Asavari sat bolt upright on the mattress.

'Arrested? For what?' Her voice quivered a little.

'I don't know the details, tai, but it seems one of the musicians was carrying marijuana in his jacket and also assaulted a girl somewhere. Now I don't know what exactly Upendra is charged with, but he has been arrested. The organization that got your visas done called just now and gave me the news. They're arranging for a lawyer for Upendra but as you can imagine they are very upset and have been advised to send you back to India as soon as possible, because the rest of the tour will have to be cancelled. They said Upendra may be deported, but they want to get you back to India safely as soon as possible. Do you understand, tai?'

Asavari looked disbelievingly at her, in complete shock. 'But, I don't even have my ticket. This Upendra had everything with him, our tickets, schedule...I have my visa and passport but everything else is with him. I only have five hundred dollars with me, because I thought I should keep at least some money. But that will not be enough for my ticket, even.'

'Don't worry, we'll all help,' Minal said, worried that the poor lady might pass out, or worse, and that was really not what they needed right now.

The next couple of days went by in a blur, and before she knew it, Asavari was headed back to India. She was unable to sleep on the flight, and slept in fits and starts even when she was back in her apartment in Pune. She was glad to be home and made herself a huge bowl of poha for breakfast. It consoled her.

Or so she thought. For when her part-time domestic help greeted her cheerfully with 'Welcome back, foreign-returned tai, what did you get for me from America?' Asavari burst into tears.

Taan Kaptaan

Vishwas Saxena had recently been re-elected General Secretary of the Meerut branch of Sangeet Sewa Samaj—SSS—a cultural organization which was, to quote from its website:

> '...dedicated to teaching only great classical music and creating a genuine network of lesser known artistes, and encouraging a non-commercial exchange of serious concert opportunities between genuinely networked members.'

To a neutral person, this might have sounded dull, not to say wordy and a little pompous. But among unsung practitioners of classical music, there was a consensus that it was a much needed project. And Saxena Sir—as he was known to his five hundred odd music students—was considered an excellent choice for General Secretary, especially as the Meerut SSS was headquartered in his home.

Saxena Sir, now in his early fifties, had led the charge for years in the city, waging a war of sorts to preserve and promote authentic classical music—'*sacchaa shaashtriya sangeet*'. He had inherited this mantle from his father, who was known among Meerut's music lovers as Bade (or Big) Sir. Bade Sir had begun his professional life by teaching sitar, Hindustani vocal music, tabla and later guitar and Casio at every hobby class in the city. In the late 1950s, he had started petitioning successive governments of Uttar Pradesh for a plot of land at subsidized rates to build a music school, and finally succeeded a decade later. On this land he constructed a two-storey building, setting up home on the first floor and a music school on the ground floor, which he named Sangeet Sewa Kendra. Here, not only did Bade Sir teach music to generations of aspiring musicians, he also groomed his son Vishwas and daughter-in-law Vaishali for a dynastic takeover when he retired. At least half a dozen of his students found placements in the school as lecturers, ad-hoc instructors and accompanists. And since he was often invited to be on various selection committees as an expert, he also installed members of his brood in the music departments of several universities, colleges and schools in the region.

Some years before he died, Bade Sir founded a not-for-profit cultural organization, the aforementioned Sangeet Sewa Samaj, 'guided' by him and run by a trust constituted of his most admiring ex-students, or their spouses, in seven cities across India. After him, the responsibility of guiding SSS fell upon his son. By this time, SSS branches in the other cities had broken away and were functioning entirely independently, sharing only the name with the parent body that Bade Sir had founded. But in Meerut it was still one happy family that ran the school and organization, and controlled most musical activity in and around the city.

Saxena Sir, as benevolent and cheerful as Bade Sir had been, pied-pipered his band of followers through the mysteries of Hindustani classical music, organizing concerts whenever he managed to extract funds from someone, appointing new teachers and authoring guide books—the popular *kunjis*—for music examinations. But despite the position of command he held, Saxena Sir longed for stardom, for name and fame—why, for instance, wasn't he invited to shows in the big cities of India, let alone Europe and America? He had hoped that his fortunes would change once he became General Secretary of SSS Meerut and could leverage at least a couple of exchange programmes by providing performance opportunities to artistes from elsewhere, who would in turn invite him to events in *their* cities. But it was not to be.

In the last five years, the only time he had performed

outside Meerut was when the Roorkee unit of SSS (a mere two hours by road) invited him to sing at their conference. And then he'd got only twenty-five minutes, because the artiste featured before him—playing classical music on the Hawaiian guitar, of all things!—exceeded the time allotted to him by a good forty minutes. To add insult to injury, the boorish fellow, who had tortured and scraped his instrument at high decibels and speeds, had elicited thunderous applause from the audience. After that, poor Saxena Sir, tense, irritated and exhausted, barely managed a quavering *alaap* in Raag Bihag, through which he had to clear his throat every few minutes for all the dust he had inhaled on the highway. Before he knew it, Bagchi from the Roorkee SSS was creeping up to him on stage to whisper that he needed to wind up, or he would have to pay the venue an additional amount for using the auditorium beyond the allotted time. Being the cooperative gentleman he was, Saxena Sir obliged, but he did whisper back to Bagchi that he hadn't even warmed up yet; it was all very unfair, to him and to the audience who had come to listen to him. At which point Bagchi drew his attention, with a sideways jerk of the head, to the rows of plastic chairs before them. They were mostly empty, the audience having thinned considerably after the fire-and-brimstone recital on the Hawaiian guitar.

Upon his return to Meerut, Saxena Sir shared his

disappointment with his wife, who counselled him, in the slow nasal drawl that was also typical of her singing: '*Baat suno, aap na, cum-po-jeeshun par concentrate karo. Gaana toh koi bhi gaa sakta hai, cum-po-jeeshun har kisi-ke bas ki baat nahin.* (Listen to me, concentrate on composing. Anyone can sing, but not everyone can be a composer.)'

Watching her husband's face crumple, she added consolingly: 'Of course, whenever you get an invitation to sing, you can always accept. But I'm telling you, it is as a composer that you will be famous.'

And so it was that Saxena Sir embarked on a journey to discover his hidden genius as a composer. He did not fail entirely this time. The father of one of his students, who was a senior officer in the Meerut Development Authority, commissioned him to compose and record an anthem for the Swachh Bharat campaign. In just three days, Saxena Sir wrote and composed what he believed was his magnum opus:

Swachh Swachh Swachh, mera Bharat hai ab Swachh!
Swachhata sangraam ko diya humne sarvaswa.

(Clean, clean, clean, our India is now clean!
To the Swachhata campaign, we've given all we have)

With twenty of his students, he then travelled to Delhi's Daryaganj to record the song at a government-approved studio. It was on a fairly large floor, with musty faded-green wall-to-wall carpeting, and a sleepy, paan-chewing recording engineer who rarely spoke, but for cryptic bursts in a hybrid of Hindi and Punjabi prefaced with expletives. Saxena Sir conducted the musicians and singers earnestly throughout the recording sessions, feet planted wide apart as he flailed his arms as though he were regulating unruly traffic. All the musicians and singers knew their parts well and needed no prompting or conducting, and they urged him to relax, but Saxena Sir, breathless and flushed, declared, '*Arre bhai, driver ke bina gaadi kaise chalegi?* (But how will a car move without a driver?)'

Exhausted, somewhat disoriented by the digital technology in use, but still full of nervous energy, Saxena Sir finally returned to Meerut armed with the Swachhta anthem on a pen drive folded into a handkerchief and sealed in a brown envelope which he carried carefully in a briefcase.

The anthem was launched with much fanfare, with top officials of the District Administration in attendance. Saxena Sir conducted his group of singers and musicians with the same comic earnestness that had been on display in the studio. The female singers in the group had opted to wear rani-pink saris bought at Meerut's most popular store, Lajja Sarees. And the men wore turquoise kurtas with white churidars and pink waistcoats. Saxena Sir wore an elaborately embroidered purple sherwani with zardozi work, teamed with a silk scarf in turquoise and pink slung over his shoulders. At one point, as he waved his arms violently, one end of the scarf got caught in the zardozi work on the sleeve of his sherwani, and for the rest of the performance, he conducted—unnecessarily, again—his students with a turquoise and pink veil shielding his right profile. It was only after the song was over that he was able to wrench the scarf away from the goldwork on his sleeve, tearing it in the process. In usual circumstances, he would have been dismayed by the accident, but this was a special occasion. And frankly, the damage done to his expensive scarf was a mere trifle compared to the compliments he received. From his student Meera Mallik's husband, for instance. This owner of Meerut's largest banquet hall came up to him, eyes shining and moist with admiration, and declared, '*Bai Gawd Sir, aap to bilkul Mojaat lag rahe the!*' (By God Sir, you looked just like Mozart!)'

It was at this launch that Saxena Sir's luck truly turned. After the anthem had been sung and Saxena Sir formally felicitated by senior, intermediate and junior district officials, tea and refreshments were announced. While the junta broke loose and swooped down on the snacks and beverages, VIPs and other local luminaries and Saxena Sir were ushered into a separate *pandal* where they would be served at tables draped in stained white tablecloths and decorated with identical arrangements of plastic flowers. The chairs around each table were dressed up in cheap white satin covers with grimy gold bows tied on the back. To begin with, Saxena Sir shared a table with the big-wigs of the Meerut Administration, solicitously passing on snacks to the sahibs and their spouses, or directing the waiters to refill their tea cups. But once the VIPs departed, he shifted to a neighbouring table that had been fiercely claimed by his wife, son (who had come especially for the big day from his engineering college in Manipal) and brood of loyal students. As he lowered himself into a chair, exhausted by the day's activities, his wife instructed one of the students to get their Sir hot tea and snacks.

Just as Saxena Sir took his first sip of the piping hot tea, and sank his teeth into a samosa, a man approached the table, bending low to greet him with a 'Namaste, Sir'. Saxena Sir scrambled to his feet, brushing samosa crumbs off the shredded scarf that he had fastened round his neck like a bib. He quickly wiped his fingers on a paper napkin he had managed to grab, before he returned the visitor's Namaste. He had no idea who the man was, but if he was in this *pandal* and not one of his students or related to any of them, he was most likely a VIP. Large, lumbering, and dressed sloppily in blue jeans and a full-sleeved maroon shirt, the visitor apologized for causing a disturbance, and urged Saxena Sir to sit down: '*Sir, aap baithiye na sir, please.*'

'Sir, my name is Ramesh Gupta,' the visitor said. 'I am a successful businessman from Delhi, but actually my true love is Hindustani classical music. Unfortunately, sir, I was born in a family which has no taste for music and arts, and I was never given the opportunity to learn music. But once I grew up and was able to take independent decisions, I started listening to music and have been an ardent listener ever since. And sir, although I could not learn myself, I am keen to do something for classical music, to help bring it to the masses. Because, sir, as you know better than me, our culture is being taken over by all this rubbish music from the West and people are forgetting the value of our traditions. We really need to do something about this, and that is why I have come to you.'

Saxena Sir stopped munching, put down his teacup, smiled like a martyr walking to the gallows, and said, 'Gupta ji, my late father and I have already committed our lives to the service of music. What more can we do? I am a small man. How can I help you?'

Ramesh Gupta replied promptly and with utmost deference, 'Sir, everyone knows about your *sangeet sewa* as well as that of Bade Sir. We cannot hope to match such dedication and sacrifice. But if you permit, someone like me can be a humble *sewak* too, sir, under your leadership.'

Not quite sure how he should respond, Saxena Sir mumbled, 'Yes, Gupta ji, of course. We need people like you.'

Encouraged, Gupta leaned forward and said, 'We should meet and plan something unique, sir. Something that is totally different, a new venture. Can we meet tomorrow, sir? At your place? I need about one hour with you to explain what I have in mind. Anytime convenient for you, sir, I will be there. Please give me just one hour and I am sure you will be convinced.'

A little confused but intrigued nevertheless, Saxena Sir invited Gupta to his home at eleven the next morning.

Gupta reached Swaralaya, the Saxena home, at eleven sharp the following morning and was welcomed into the living room. He settled into one of the maroon rexine sofas and fidgeted while Mrs Saxena made a great fuss about serving him tea and biscuits. He waited for her to settle down, before launching into a detailed account of his plan, for which he solicited the active support and participation of Saxena Sir and his family.

'Sir,' he began, 'I want to launch a talent hunt, a nation-wide hunt for the best talent in classical music. And this must be done as professionally and as slickly as are the talent hunts for popular music, you know, "Sa Re Ga Ma" or "Indian Idol" or "Chhote Ustad". Sir, if you are the man behind this talent hunt, it will be taken seriously because everyone knows what Bade Sir and you have done for classical music in this region. Sir, first we have to make an announcement about the talent hunt with full-on, *dhaansu* publicity. I want to rope in some brand ambassadors for this, like film stars who have an interest in classical music and dance. Maybe Hema Malini ji, or Sharmila ji or even, if we are lucky, Vidya Balan. Top stars from films, sir, no Tulsi-Phulsi, Anandi-Shanandi television types. Only big stars—that's how we'll launch the contest. Every contestant will have to buy an application form to be able to participate. And each form will cost a thousand rupees, one thousand only. So, if we get ten thousand applications from all parts of the country, we'll get one crore straightaway. And this is apart from the sponsorship amounts I will get for this project. I'll get sponsorship, sir. You don't worry about that. God willing, I should be able to arrange sponsorship to the tune of ten-twelve crores. But you must try and get as many people as possible to apply.'

Saxena Sir, sitting across from Gupta, listened in silence, the expression on his face shifting from surprise to bewilderment to complete astonishment, even alarm. In the world of classical music, a crore was not a familiar figure. When he wanted to raise funds for his institution or for a music project, he grovelled and whined for as little as ten thousand rupees from each sponsor. And here was this man talking so casually of raising ten-twelve crores! Was it really that simple? A strange new excitement, a fearful thrill of doing something illicit, made his heart beat faster. To calm himself, he began to hum a Surdas bhajan.

'Sir, so should I go ahead?' Gupta asked.

Before Saxena Sir could answer, his wife, who had so far been a silent witness, cut in, '*Achha* Gupta ji, what time would you like to have lunch?'

When Gupta said politely that he would leave before lunch, she was indignant. '*Arre! Aisa kaise ho sakta hai, Bhai sahab?* (How can that be, Bhai sahab?) No no, you will have to eat with us, whatever little *rookhi-sookhi* daal-roti-chutney we are able to offer you. I will not take no for an answer. Both of you go ahead with your discussion, I will organize some lunch and be back in a few minutes.' She gathered the empty tea cups, and on her way out, said to her husband, '*Suniye* (Listen).' Saxena Sir excused himself and followed her obediently to the kitchen.

Once they were safely out of earshot, she turned around and said, 'Listen to me now—don't you go and agree to anything he asks you to do without first discussing a fee. He's clearly a shrewd fellow and knows how to make money, so why should you not get any?'

Mr Saxena mumbled uncertainly, 'It's too early to ask him about money...I mean, let me at least find out what I have to do...at the right moment I will discuss money with him.'

'No,' said his wife firmly. 'You will not. Wait for me to return to the room and I will handle this, otherwise I know what you will do—sit there like the cat got your tongue and let this fellow talk you into doing anything he wants without paying so much as a paisa out of those crores he's bragging about. Don't you dare!'

'*Achha achha*, you do the talking, *Bhaagwan*. Let me return to him now, what will he think?'

Over lunch—daal, raita, two *sabzis*, rice and a cucumber-onion salad—on a small round dining table covered with a plastic sheet, a deal was brokered between Gupta and the Saxenas. The Saxenas would handle the musical part of the project, spread the word about the contest, hire the necessary musicians and instruments, arrange for stage, sound, lights, etc, and use their contacts to persuade star musicians to judge the contest gratis, if possible, or for very little money. Gupta would handle the marketing and any other aspects that Saxena Sir was uncertain about. All profits would be shared equally, and Gupta assured them a minimum of two crores.

'God willing,' Gupta said as they moved from the dining table back to the rexine sofas, 'it could even be more.'

At this point, Mrs Saxena, her heart beating as steadily as it always did—unlike her husband's, which was racing again—asked: 'Will there be a contract?'

'*Ji bhabhi ji, bilkul*,' Gupta replied. 'Of course there will be a contract. Let's just work out the details of the agreement and then we can get a lawyer to draw up a contract. In fact, you can get the contract drawn up by your own lawyer if you feel more confident with that arrangement.'

'No, no, Bhai sahab, if you have a good lawyer we can ask him. *Yeh toh bahut seedhe hain* (He's just too straight and simple),' she said, referring to her husband. 'He doesn't know a thing about law-shaw.'

'Don't worry, Bhabhi ji, *main hoon na*. I will handle all this. After all, Sir is an artiste, he shouldn't have to bother with lowly business matters. And Bhabhi ji, I understand your concern. You must think that I'm one of those *chaalu* people who try to take advantage of sadhu-like artistes like our Sir. But please don't worry, I'm not that kind of person. In fact, even though we have not signed an agreement, I would like to start our association by offering Sir a token amount of fifty-one thousand rupees for his time and patience.'

Gupta reached for the small black leather pouch he always carried with him, unzipped it, withdrew a wad of notes and thrust it at Saxena Sir, who stared incredulously at Gupta for a few seconds and then looked at his wife accusingly for doubting Gupta's intentions. She shifted a little in her sofa, and cleared her throat to hide her confusion. With the magnanimity of a victor, Gupta now turned to Mrs Saxena and thrust the wad of notes at her. She took it, but to deny Gupta complete satisfaction, did not speak the obligatory words for such an occasion: '*Arre, iski kya zaroorat thi Bhai sahab*...(There was no need for this at all, Bhai sahab...).' She accepted the token amount without a word and stood up as Gupta did to take his leave: '*Achha Sir, Bhabi ji, phir haazir hota hoon.* (Okay Sir, Bhabi ji, I'll present myself again soon.)'

Late that evening, after Mrs Saxena had finished the day's chores, the couple were finally able to sit together and speak to each other in the privacy of their room. Both were excited, but Mrs Saxena remained wary of Gupta. Her husband chided her, saying, '*Tum na, khaam-a-kha shaq karti ho logon par.* (You know, you are suspicious of everyone for no rhyme or reason.)'

'*Aur aap na, sudhrenge nahin aur log aap ke bholepan ka faayda uthaate rahenge* (And you will remain a simpleton and continue to let people take advantage of you),' Mrs Saxena shot back. 'I'll say this a hundred times if I have to: you can't be a sadhu with everyone. You should keep a strict watch on this Gupta. Don't be swayed just because he has given us a little money upfront.'

Soon Gupta became a regular visitor at the Saxena home. Sometimes he arrived unannounced to discuss urgent plans and stayed on for meals. Or he called several times a day. As the planning for the project hurtled forward at breakneck speed, Mrs Saxena too was caught up in the excitement, dropped any reservations she may have harboured about Gupta's intentions, and became an ally. She did not, however, fail to remind Gupta at regular intervals about the contract he and her husband were to sign. Gupta responded earnestly to all her reminders, jotting down points to be included in the contract, or bringing up issues that required further discussion and clarification.

And then, as the signing of the contract seemed imminent, the matter was forgotten, as the first of a series of differences of opinion arose between Saxena Sir and Gupta. Before any papers could be signed and potential sponsors approached, before any announcement could be made, they needed a name for the talent hunt. Saxena Sir came up with not one but five names: *Raag Rang, Parampara, Sur Sewa, Sur Sadhna, Sangeet Tapasya*. All of these were immediately rejected by Gupta.

'*Sir, in mein se koi bhi nahin chalega*. (None of these will work.) Sir, we can't have such old-fashioned names. We need something for the youth, something that will make them feel classical music is also rocking. Something like, like—' he shut his eyes to indicate he was thinking hard, and then snapped his fingers—'*Raagon ka Rasiya!*'

'*Hain? Kya?* (What?)' Saxena Sir exclaimed in shock and indignation. '*Raagon ka Rasiya? Raagon ka* Rasiya! *Vaahiyaat!* (That's vulgar!)' And then, surprised by his display of anger and keen to preserve his image of a sadhu-like man, a down-to-earth artiste, he said reasonably, '*Zara sochiye Gupta ji, hum shaastriya sangeet ki baat kar rahe hain, pop music ki nahin.* (Do consider, Gupta ji, we are speaking of classical music, not pop music.) Besides, *rasiya* is a term used for a male. Won't there be any women in this contest? What will you call them? If you want something simpler and easy to remember, why not *Sargam ki Talaash?* It is musical and also accurate. We are looking for the very essence of music, are we not?'

Gupta wasn't giving in. 'But Sargam is a term for neither males nor females, sir. At least that is what I think, and most people are like me, sir, very ignorant.'

'Then let us say *Talaash-e-Sargam* or *Sargam ka Sartaj* or *Sushri aur Shri Sargam ki Talaash*,' said Saxena Sir, and when Gupta groaned and clutched his head, hastened to add, 'or maybe just *Miss aur Master Sargam ki Talaash?* I think that is also modern. It will also sound okay in English, you know: "The search for Miss and Master Sargam", no?'

Gupta tried another tack. 'It is too long, sir.'

'Gupta ji, you don't like anything I'm suggesting,' complained Saxena Sir.

'Okay, sir,' Gupta sighed, 'let us go with your last suggestion. But can we shorten it? MM-SKIT...it might work.'

'*Hain? Maine aisa toh kuchh nahin kahaa.* (But I never suggested anything of the sort.)'

'Short form, sir, like DDLJ. MM-SKIT for *Miss aur Master Sargam ki Talaash*. Short and modern—actually, it is also musical.'

'What's DDLJ?' asked a baffled Saxena Sir.

'*Arre*, sir, *Dilwale Dulhaniya Le Jayenge*. Haven't you seen the movie? Everyone has seen it.'

'No no, absolutely not. On the one hand you want to promote classical music, and on the other, you want to make everything filmi. I cannot agree to this, Gupta ji.'

A tense silence descended, and squatted like a grey cloud between them. Finally, after a minute or so, Gupta said, 'Okay, sir, we can ask the PR agency to suggest something. Let us not worry. But sir, you have given me a great idea! We need some judges who will appeal to serious music lovers and the general audience as well—to young and old, traditional and modern. You remember Miss Sargam, sir? She was so big as a pop singer but she gave it all up and returned to her first love, which was classical music. Even your organization gave her an award for her classical singing. Remember, sir?'

Saxena Sir nodded. He had never thought much of that pop-star turned Sangeet Samragyi, Empress of Music. But it was his father, then past eighty, who had given her the award in a weak moment, so Saxena Sir had always kept his disapproval to himself.

'Sir, it would be fantastic for our show if we could have her as a judge for the finale,' Gupta said. 'Do you know where she lives now? She seems to have disappeared. *Bharat ki Mystery Kokila ek baar phir duniya ke saamne—PR ke liye bhi perfect hoga sir.* (India's mystery nightingale returns. It will be perfect for PR, too.)'

'No, Gupta ji. I have no information about the lady you mention. I can bring you the other judges, but I would request you to take the responsibility of looking for Miss Sargam upon yourself.'

'No problem, sir. I always love a challenge! Okay, sir, I will see you tomorrow.'

But Gupta was back the same evening. The PR agency had come up with a few names that were, variously, folksy, whimsical, modern and sophisticated. For a while Saxena Sir and Gupta found it difficult to agree on any of the names, and it seemed the talent hunt idea would end up being a non-starter. Then, fortunately, Mrs Saxena weighed in on the folksy option—'Taan Kaptaan'—and a crisis was averted. 'It has the fragrance of both *shaastriya sangeet* (classical music) and *lok sangeet* (folk music),' she said. 'It will make serious music lovers happy because Ustad Fateh Ali Khan sahab was famous by this name. And it also sounds light enough to appeal to young people.' And so a crisis was averted. The project was titled Taan Kaptaan, or Captain of the Taan, to denote a person who has mastered the art of singing *taans*. Saxena Sir was happy and Gupta too decided he could live with the title, though he would have preferred 'NexGen Ustads', one of the other options the PR agency had given them.

The project gathered speed again. Hoardings appeared in Meerut, Delhi, Lucknow and neighbouring cities announcing the contest in Hindi and English:

> *India ka pehla classical talent hunt—Taan Kaptaan!*
> India's very first classical talent hunt—Taan Kaptaan!

A selection of SSS students learning music from Guru Vishwas Saxena were featured in all the publicity with the catch line, '*Bharat ki kalaa, Bharat ki dharohar. Kya aap banenge Bharat ke naye Taan Kaptaan?* (The art of India, the treasure of India. Will you be India's new Taan Kaptaan?)' A telephone number and website address were provided for further details. The Saxenas and their students went from one hoarding to another, posed in front of each and promptly posted the pictures on Facebook with captions like: '*Hum aur hamare Saxena Sir, shaastriya sangeet ki sewa mein!* (With our very own

Saxena Sir, in the service of classical music!)' Meanwhile, Gupta arranged to have small handouts of the Taan Kaptaan contest slipped in with the morning newspapers that vendors delivered to every subscriber. A buzz was successfully created around the show and within a week 1000 contestants had paid for the application form, and over 800 applications had been submitted. In the second week, more application forms were purchased and more applications submitted.

Encouraged by the auspicious start to the project, Saxena Sir started calling gurus and music schools in different parts of the country to inform them about the contest and the role he was playing. Meanwhile, Gupta followed up on his contacts in the corporate world and requested meetings with them to solicit their support in the venture. Although the marketing managers of most businesses had no taste for classical music, and saw Gupta and his project as a bit of a nuisance, some of them found the 'heritage' aspect of the project a good fit for their products and marketing strategies. Apsara Kaajal had for years aggressively advertised its 'age-old' methods of making kaajal with the purest of ingredients and formulas invented by the sages, the *rishis* and *munis*, of the Vedic era. Classical music too was a product of Vedic knowledge, argued Gupta, and thus got Apsara Kaajal to cough up twenty-five lakhs for the talent hunt. There were others who followed suit: Heritage Sarees, Ashwagandha Hair Oil, Arya Computers and Saraswati notebooks. Gupta played his hand well, and enthused by his success, Saxena Sir reached out to classical music institutes and clubs across the country, and lo and behold, the show managed to get 15,000 applications in less than a month.

Gupta declared it was action time, and forged ahead with implementing the show format that Saxena Sir and he had developed over many weeks of arguing and discussing. Each applicant was allotted a roll number to ensure that complete impartiality was maintained in the first round of screening. A letter was sent out by speed post to every applicant with the allotted roll number and a request to send a recording on a CD or a pen drive of renditions in any two raags of their choice. Saxena Sir insisted that every applicant be asked to send a rendition each in one morning raag and one evening raag. A deadline for the submission of recordings was provided, and those who missed the deadline would automatically be barred from participating in the contest.

Packets with CDs and pen drives started arriving and Gupta arranged to have them stacked and locked carefully in trunks for the screening that would take place in a month, after the deadline for submissions expired. It became apparent to both him and Saxena Sir that this was going to be a mammoth task that would require them to be well-staffed, organized, cautious, and vigilant at all times. But they were on a high, and no challenge seemed too big. 'Sir,' said Gupta one day, 'I feel that the world is at our feet. We are making history, and all because of you, sir.' To which Saxena Sir replied, uncharacteristically, in English—something he did only in moments of high excitement—'I also am feeling on top of the world, Gupta ji, only because of you!'

At the Sangeet Sewa Samaj office, courier boys rang the bell through the day to deliver packages, and anxious participants and their guardians constantly followed up on the phone to ask if their submissions had reached. But this soon became a nuisance—as the SSS office, the music school and the Saxena residence were all housed in the same building, each time the couriers rang the bell, someone from the family had to rush down to the ground floor to sign for and accept the package. This task fell to the lady of the house, because the lord and master could not possibly be inconvenienced, and for several days Mrs Saxena, being a devoted spouse, dropped whatever she was doing to rush down the stairs to sign for and accept the CDs and pen drives. It didn't matter if she had just started lunch or was in the middle of the daily phone conversation with her son in Manipal, or if she was taking a power nap after having cooked and cleaned and taken the post-lunch music class. If the doorbell rang, it was she who would go down to answer it. But in a few days even *her* patience ran out, and fed up of running up and down the stairs all day she finally slammed a CD on the table in front of her husband and said, '*Bas, bahut ho gaya!* (I've had enough!) I can't keep doing this all day, day after day. You have to hire someone else to look after all this nonsense, or get Gupta to give his address for submissions.'

Gupta was promptly summoned, and with characteristic slickness he found a quick and effective solution. He installed a guard at the gate of the building to accept all courier packets and apologized profusely to Mrs Saxena. 'Bhabhi ji,' he said, with folded hands, 'please forgive me. I should have thought of you and realized how much trouble we are causing.'

A week after the deadline for submitting entries expired, Gupta arranged for a jury, selected by Saxena Sir, to assemble for the first phase of screening and shortlisting of the recordings that had been submitted. Three teams of five jury members each, all from Meerut, were assigned the task of screening the 6,326 CDs that had been submitted. They gathered every day from 10 am to 5 pm, six days a week, at three rooms provided by the Saxenas' music school—the Sangeet Sewa Kendra—to listen to the recordings and shortlist five hundred applicants. Tea, coffee, biscuits, snacks and lunch were provided to them every day along with a small monthly honorarium for their services. They were asked to observe confidentiality about the process and their own roles in it, but of course it wasn't long before just about everyone in Meerut knew all there was to know about the screening and selections. Sly phone calls were made to the Saxenas by dozens of cousins, uncles, aunties, friends and acquaintances, ostensibly to exchange pleasantries or make some innocent enquiries about the courses offered by Sangeet Sewa Kendra, but within minutes pretences were dropped and the callers would reveal their real agenda of approach *lagaana,* or using 'influence' to get Saxena Sir to ensure that the candidates they were supporting were shown special favours in the selection process. The more aggressive and resourceful would go a step further and land up at Sangeet Sewa Kendra unannounced to petition him in person. Ultimately, the guard Gupta had stationed at the gate to accept courier packets was given additional charge of keeping all such petitioners at bay.

For a brief period, alarm bells rang in Mrs Saxena's mind, reminding her that the much-discussed contract between her husband and Gupta still remained unsigned. But when she brought this up, Saxena Sir silenced her with an accusatory glare and a stern admonition. 'Shalu, if you continue to be so suspicious of everyone and everything, you are going to turn into a *khadoos* old woman. Stop being such a nag. Rarely do you find people who are so willing to support classical music, and when they turn up at your doorstep offering to help, all you can do is suspect them. I don't like this attitude. Gupta ji is working so hard, he's bringing in all the money on his own, and yet we will get an equal share. He's being more than fair.'

Though slightly chastened, Mrs Saxena argued that while all of that might be true, it was also true that they were providing rooms for the screening process and should be compensated for that. Saxena Sir left the room in a huff, saying she should present a bill to Gupta for renting the rooms. '*Theek hai*, that is exactly what I'll do,' declared Mrs Saxena, 'and don't you interfere when I do!'

And indeed she did bring up the issue with Gupta when he showed up next. Gupta showed no surprise or displeasure whatsoever, and only asked her to suggest an amount she considered reasonable for the hiring of the three rooms. There was, however, a cold edge to his voice when he responded to her promptly proffered suggestion of ten thousand rupees a month per room: 'Okay, Bhabhi ji,' he said, 'if that is what you think is reasonable, I will send thirty thousand for one month. And rest assured that if the screening carries on beyond one month, I will send the same amount for the next month too.'

It took the selectors forty-five days of serious sifting to go through all the CDs and pen drives, discard those that were damaged or would not play, and then select five hundred that they felt made the mark for the first round. The names of the five hundred applicants were announced with some fanfare at a function held at the Town Hall in Meerut which was presided over by a Judge of the District Court. Saxena Sir's students belted out a Saraswati Vandana and then, for reasons unclear to the audience, his Swachhata anthem as well. Praise was heaped upon Saxena Sir and Gupta for preserving and promoting the true heritage of India. Both accepted the over-the-top compliments with a matching display of exaggerated humility, and the contest moved on towards its next milestone.

The five hundred applicants selected in the first round were sent letters and text messages asking them to prepare for the second round by presenting themselves in Delhi for a video shoot which would be financed in equal parts by the organizers of the talent hunt and the participants themselves. Each participant was asked to contribute thirty thousand rupees, and a matching amount would be provided by the organizers. Those who agreed to these terms would be provided professional facilities to shoot a performance video. All videos shot in this round were to be uploaded on YouTube and a new jury of five members would select fifty contestants for the final round of the contest.

At this juncture, the two brains behind Taan Kaptaan found themselves in disagreement with each other once again. Saxena Sir felt that thirty thousand rupees would be unaffordable for many candidates, especially as travel, boarding and lodging costs were not included in this amount. Gupta argued that the culture of freebies was what devalued classical music and its exponents, and that paying for the application form and then for this round of video shooting would assign a certain value and professionalism to the project. Saxena was forced to concede defeat in the matter when several selected contestants and their guardians promptly queued up to pay, showing little or no resistance to the demand for funds. Ultimately, 376 candidates submitted their contributions of thirty thousand rupees each, which added up to over a crore and twelve lakhs of rupees. And Gupta got a fresh sponsor to deposit a matching amount in the bank account he had opened for the contest.

Saxena Sir was also concerned about the time required to shoot the videos. He had been told that it would be several months before all the videos had been shot, edited and uploaded, and he felt this could lead to a decline in general interest in the contest. He was of the opinion that the performances of the 376 applicants should take place simultaneously at four or five centres across the country, like Mumbai, Kolkata, Bengaluru, Delhi and perhaps

Bhopal, and that each of the performances should be televised serially as in any regular talent show. Gupta explained that televising the performances in multiple cities would be very expensive and it would be difficult, if not impossible, to find adequate long-term sponsorship for a programme of classical music. He wanted only the final fifty applicants to be on television, and counter-argued that to raise money even for that final televised round, he needed the months that it would take to film, edit and upload the performances of the 376 applicants who had been selected.

Saxena Sir was unconvinced. 'Don't we have enough money, Gupta ji?' he asked. 'I mean, you have raised some six-seven crores, haven't you? Can't we use some of that money for televising? Why don't you and I sit and make a budget—after keeping our share aside, of course.'

Once again, Gupta gave in. He asked for a couple of days to go over the budget carefully. 'We can then see if we have the money to start televising the performances in this second round itself.'

'*Chalo theek hai*, no problem,' said Saxena Sir.

'Okay, sir, I will see you two days from now,' said Gupta as he walked down the stairs and out of the house.

That was the last time Saxena Sir set eyes upon Ramesh Gupta. For two days no one suspected that something was amiss, because Gupta had already said he needed that long to work on the estimates. But when he did not show up on the third and fourth days and when there was no call from him, either, Mrs Saxena raised the alarm.

'*Suniye*,' she said to her husband, 'where is your friend Gupta? We don't see him around these days. Have you two had a fight?'

'Don't be silly, Shalu,' said Saxena Sir, 'you know well I don't fight. Gupta ji must be busy working on the estimate for the multi-city television show. It is not a simple business.'

But when a week passed, Saxena Sir began to worry. And then he began to panic, for calls to both of Gupta's phone numbers received the identical automated answer: '*Yeh number astitva mein nahin hai*. This number does *not* exist.' Emissaries were sent to Gupta's address in Meerut, only to find the door locked. In despair, Saxena Sir finally apprised his wife of the situation and asked, '*Shalu, yeh sab kya ho gaya? Yeh Gupta kahan gaayab ho gaya? Hum kya karenge, Shalu?* (What is this, Shalu, what has happened? Where has this Gupta disappeared? What will we do now, Shalu?)'

Mrs Saxena was unable to console him, because she knew that they were in serious trouble. Her fears had come true. Gupta was a conman who had bolted with all the money he had managed to collect for the show, and now they would have to face the music. 'Let's go and meet your friends in the police force and administration,' she said, trying to appear calm. 'They will be able to advise us. Give me the numbers, I will speak to them and request appointments.'

As she made the calls, Saxena Sir sat on the edge of their bed, head in his hands. In the weeks that followed, the Saxenas saw a flurry of activity involving meetings with politicians, bureaucrats, police officials and lawyers. The couple were well known and respected in Meerut and had a large following, and everyone was sympathetic and eager to help. But the situation was undeniably grave. A fraud worth several crores had been committed by the two organizers of the show, one of whom was Saxena Sir. The other, namely Ramesh Gupta, was missing. Even as the politicians and policemen listened to the Saxenas, offered them tea and sympathy, they knew it wasn't worth their while to intervene, because things didn't look good at all. Poor Saxena Sir was a good man, they respected him, but he wasn't important enough for them to risk controversy. There really was no option; Saxena Sir would have to face the consequences, at least for some time. They would do what they could for him legally.

It wasn't long before news of the scam began to appear in the media, and soon dozens of complaints, FIRs and court cases were filed against the organizers by applicants and their guardians. Some of these complaints and FIRs were of cheating and fraud, and despite all the help and support the Saxenas garnered and received, Saxena Sir was ultimately arrested. When the police came to take him away, as respectfully as they could do such a thing on a hot and busy day, Mrs Saxena tried to appear dignified, although her lower lip began to tremble and her eyes filled up. But not one to give up easily, she composed her thoughts quickly and told her husband as she accompanied him down the stairs and up to the police jeep: '*Suniye, aap ghabraiye nahin, hum bail ki application daalenge jaldi se jaldi.* (Listen, don't worry, we will apply for bail at the earliest.)'

Saxena Sir, shell shocked at the thought of being in jail, utterly confused and helpless in the face of such a cruel twist of fate, looked at his devoted wife and said, 'Shalu, sorry. I should have listened to you. Had I done so, I would not be in this situation today. Please forgive me for putting you through this.'

A lock of greying hair fell over his forehead as he shook his head from side to side, slowly, sorrowfully, and then he was bundled into the jeep and taken away. A crowd of students and followers wiped away tears at the sight of what had befallen their beloved Sir. On the other side of the street stood a motley group of bystanders, loafers and onlookers, one of whom decided to provide background music to the cheerless scene by singing tunelessly—with neither *sur* nor *taal*—the R.D. Burman hit from *Amar Prem*: 'Yeh kya hua, kaise hua, kab hua, kyun hua...'

A Farewell to Music

It was a mid-winter morning in Kolkata, and although it was a bone-chilling 25 degrees Celsius and only half-past-ten, the city was fully awake. At India Musica, the country's oldest and most influential music company, it was time for an important meeting.

Founded in 1909 as India Record House, the company had quickly become a household name. For over a century, almost every classical singer and musician had recorded with IRH, and for half a century—till its monopoly ended in the 1980s—it had owned every Hindi and Bengali film song. There was competition now, but India Musica—the new name acquired at the turn of the millennium—was still one of the biggest and most prestigious brands in the business. Its annual turnover was hundreds of crores of rupees, and the 'Conference Corner' of the head office, despite the understated name, was every inch the corporate board room: large, luxurious, with wall-to-wall carpeting, polished mahogany panelling, and a huge battleship of a table running down the length of the room with plush leather chairs placed around it. Tasteful paintings by leading artists adorned the walls of the room, which was equipped with the latest lighting and light management systems. For today's meeting, notepads and freshly sharpened pencils were ready and waiting for each attendee, along with a bottle of mineral water and a glass that was covered, in a nice old-world touch, with a beaded cloth. Plain, functional rexine chairs were arranged in a row behind the plush leather ones, for assistants and lesser mortals who would be required to wait upon and assist the big shots.

Mrigo looked around for place cards, found none, and finally lowered himself into one of the modest chairs in the second row. He chose a seat in a corner of the room, where he hoped he could remain unnoticed; he did not wish to be a participant, only an observer. But the chair he had selected wanted only to be left alone. The moment he lowered himself into it, the chair let out a long, complaining fart. Startled and deeply embarrassed, he shot up, looked around and was grateful there was only one other person in the hall, an attendant at the other end of the room, polishing a door handle, who appeared not to have heard. Mrigo was reminded of a grand uncle, a safari-suited eminence who, in the middle of a conversation, would casually lean sideways on the sofa, lift an enormous buttock and release a loud and surprisingly tuneful fart. No one ever seemed to notice and the conversation continued without interruption. The one time that young Mrigo had giggled, the eminence had looked at him, laughed and said, 'It is *uttom baatkorm. Uttom sreni,* my child. The highest category of farts, no smell at all. It is an art, comes with practice.' Mrigo wasn't sure people in this board room would appreciate the art. He walked to the opposite end of the room and found himself another chair. But this one complained in exactly the tone and register of the previous chair. 'Uff!' said Mrigo, and shot up again. This won't do, he thought. He would just stand in his corner. Then two office assistants entered the room with piles of cushions and proceeded to place one on every rexine chair. '*Bosho,*' said one of them to Mrigo. 'Don't worry, it won't speak now. Sit, sit.' Relieved, Mrigo settled himself on the cushion, which sighed politely under him and then was silent.

In a few minutes, a group of men and one woman arrived and chose their seats at the table, exchanging greetings with cool, management-school confidence. Liveried attendants in spotless white suddenly appeared, as if by magic, to serve tea, coffee and snacks while a few harrowed assistants hovered solicitously around their respective bosses. Most of the men in the leather chairs were in formal suits and ties. The Mont Blanc star blazed prominently from their pockets.

The only lady in the room wore a short black skirt, an ivory-coloured shirt with a cape collar, and pointy-toe pumps. Understated jewellery, that declared itself expensive in a quiet but unmissable way, and a Swiss watch completed her ensemble. The subtlety stopped at her neck, though; the face was heavily made up in at least three different shades of peach and two of pink. The gravel in her deep voice and her stained teeth suggested she was given to smoking heavily. She had perched herself on the edge of the conference table, and was talking to a young man in a sharp blue suit, swinging her legs gently as she talked to him. Mrigo couldn't quite catch what they were discussing, but there seemed to be a flirtatious tone to their conversation, which the lady punctuated intermittently with a gasp, a wink, an arched eyebrow.

Another man seated across from them cut into their conversation suddenly, announcing: 'I believe the boss is on his way up. Should we all take our seats perhaps?'

The lady slid off the table, the men straightened their ties and patted their hair into place, and everyone hurried to the seats that had now been assigned to them, with name cards—complete with designations—placed neatly in front of each chair. The door opened and they stood up to greet a short, slightly built man in an expensive charcoal-coloured suit and red tie, who walked into the room briskly with an air of authority. Mrigo recognized the dapper man: Deepak Daga, scion of the Daga business empire who also headed India Musica.

Greeting everyone with a smile, Daga began by saying, 'Good morning, good morning. It's great to be back with all of you. Are we ready for the meeting? Let's tackle the agenda first and then we can party as much as we want to. Okay, so who's going to chair? My suggestion would be to ask Mucky to chair. I mean, he's running the company, so it's logical that he should chair the meeting.'

'Sir, no sir, please sir,' exclaimed a balding, bespectacled gent in his late fifties. 'Not me sir. It will be best if you take the Chair sir.' Mrigo wondered why Daga had called this mild, middle-aged man Mucky, but then he glanced at the name card in front of the gent. It read 'Sukanto Mukherji'. Even so—Mucky?? Mrigo felt offended on Mukherjee's behalf, but the man himself appeared not to mind at all. He was genuinely deferential, and Daga's affection seemed genuine too, if a little boarding-school.

Poor Mucky's gentle protests were swiftly silenced by his smiling boss with 'We all insist, Mucky. Now come on.' And he reluctantly shuffled to the head of the table to chair the meeting.

Sukanto Mukherji seemed well acquainted with the responsibilities of chairing such a meeting, and completed all the formalities with practised ease and efficiency. The signatures, the verification and acceptance of the minutes of the previous meeting, the resolutions were all dealt with briskly and promptly, but Mrigo had begun to feel dangerously sleepy already. He tried hard not to doze off but it was a struggle, until his ears pricked up when the next item on the agenda was announced: to discuss the way forward and vision plan for India Musica. This should be interesting, Mrigo thought, as he sat up from the slump he had folded himself into.

Mukherji began by saying, 'Sir, you have to guide us because we have found there is a perception that India Musica is an old-fashioned music label, with an interest only in classical or then mainstream film music.' Mukherji spoke fluent English, with not the smallest trace of a Bengali accent, except when it came to names. 'Sir,' he went on, 'we have to try and include some modern music, do some social media campaign and try and convince people that we are in step with the times. Sir, to do so we have added to our team one indie music specialist, Mr Roghu Aim.' Mukherji pointed towards the only man in the group who was dressed casually, in denim trousers, checked shirt and corduroy jacket. Daga and Raghu M. shook hands and exchanged introductory pleasantries: 'Welcome, glad to have you on the team.' 'Thank you, sir. Honour to be part of this great music label' and so on.

Mukherji now directed Daga's attention to the sole female member of the team. 'Sir, happy to introduce you to Miss Tawneeka Tollvaar, our special projects expert. With these two young members joining our team, I feel we will find a solution very soon and establish, or rather I would say, re-establish India Musica as the number one music label of India.' Introductions over, Mukherji invited Tanika Talwar to share her plans for the India Musica catalogue with the team.

Tanika chose to begin by crossing her long legs, smoothing her skirt down, and flicking her hair back with a flash of her painted nails. She began speaking animatedly with a childish lisp, punctuating her sentences frequently with a smile, or a wink, or a flick of the hair.

'First,' she said, 'I'd reely reely like to say how excited I am to be at India Musica, so thank you, thank you, thank you. Okay (smile and wink), now that's done, here are some of the ideas I'd like to share with yo-all, and please give me your feedback and suggestions. To begin with, sir (smile flashed Daga-wards), Mr Mukherji showed me your existing catalogue and my first thought was that its awesome, and a lot can be done to sort of, you know, reinvent it and repackage it. So of course, I still need to go through the catalogue carefully, after which I can perhaps make like a (hair flick) proper presentation. But like, I saw you have a lot of guzzles on your catalogue.'

The team looked a little confused. Mrigo giggled but quickly masked it with a cough. Unaware or uncaring of either the confusion or the mirth she had caused, Tanika chirped on, 'So now you see these guzzles have been recorded by great artistes. But the problem is that today's music lover doesn't know about these great artistes, with all due respect (hair flick), and I'm reely sorry if I offend any of you with this statement.'

The gentlemen laughed indulgently at her charming candour, and Tanika immediately put a hand over her mouth in a mock gesture of silencing herself. 'Sometimes I'm too frank! Sorreee,' she said in a little-girl squeak. Daga nodded indulgently. 'Honestly,' she continued, 'Sir, honestly speaking, we need to get these guzzle artistes into the limelight again. I mean, everyone knows of Jagjit Singh and all, but you have so many others. So I was planning to speak to a liquor brand like S & S Rare, the Scotch brand, you know (hair flick), or something like that, to put in some money to support a project that we could call "The Great Guzzle Mix by S & S" or "Guzzling with S & S—The Ultimate Mix". And I'd get a DJ to mix the guzzles in a new-age format, you know. If you ask me, I'd get DJ Dahshat to mix the project, but that's because I'm a total fan of his work. Of course, I'm not a music person, just an ideas person (smile and wink).'

She had managed to catch Daga's attention for sure.

Mukherji too was smiling benignly at his protégée's brilliance. As for the rest, Raghu M. was doodling to show his disinterest, but the majority definitely appeared very much in favour of 'guzzling'.

There was only one dissenting voice—that of Sandeep Solapurkar, a senior and experienced member of the India Musica Artists and Repertoire team, who had almost singlehandedly developed a magnificent classical music catalogue for the label. At sixty-eight, he was the oldest employee of India Record House/India Musica. The grand patriarch of the Daga empire had hired Solapurkar, a young scholar of music at Viswa Bharati, back in 1970, after reading an article he had written on the history of the sarangi. A music enthusiast whose ambition to be a sitar player had been squashed by his merchant father, the patriarch had great regard for musicians and music scholars. So fond had he grown of Solapurkar that he had extracted a promise from his sons that Solapurkar would be allowed to work at the music company for life. The sons—of whom Deepak Daga was the youngest—had kept their promise. Naturally, Solapurkar was a respected figure in the company, and, naturally, a little pompous.

'Ms. Talwar,' said Solapurkar now, gravely, in a beautiful baritone, 'your enthusiasm is commendable. But I'm afraid I am in total disagreement with your plans. We have recorded artistes like the great Begum Akhtar. You can't possibly desecrate her music with this new-age plan you have come up with. It would be blasphemous and quite frankly, we would lose all credibility with connoisseurs of music. Mr Daga, you cannot allow this plan to go ahead. I beg you not to encourage it.'

Daga had every intention of encouraging the plan, but in a conciliatory tone he explained to Solapurkar: 'Now, now, let's not get agitated, Sandeep da. Let's keep an open mind and encourage the youngsters who have joined our team. We may not always agree with the projects put up for our consideration, but let's at least listen to the voices of youth. I'm told they are half the country now! So they are the bosses, and in any case, we must be democratic.'

'But Mr Daga, I have always supported young artistes, always,' protested Solapurkar.

'Exactly, Sandeep da,' Daga agreed. 'You have also supported innovation. Who can forget that only a few years ago you were responsible for one of our highest-selling solo albums? Who would have thought a lady dressed in a three-piece suit and hat, singing in both male and female voices and mixing pop and classical would be such a hit! But there she was, Miss Sargam—remember? She was your discovery. That's the kind of innovative material we're looking for, Sandeep da.'

'Well, that was different. Someone like her won't be

easy to find. She knew her music, and she never took such atrocious liberties.' And here Solapurkar waved his hand in the general direction of Tanika Talwar, without looking at her.

'Indeed, Sandeep da,' Daga said. 'We certainly shouldn't take too many liberties. I agree with you one hundred per cent that we must not touch Begum Akhtar's recordings. But we can mix other ghazal artistes, or at least do a pilot mix on some tracks, can't we? Let's see how the PR and marketing teams respond to the idea and the music, and then we can take a call according to their recommendations. Is that acceptable, Sandeep da?'

Solapurkar had been in the company long enough to know when not to push his luck with the ultimate boss. But he also knew that too visible a surrender in public could be damaging to one's image. Silence was usually the best policy in such a situation. He pursed his lips and poured himself a glass of water.

Deepak Daga continued, 'Excellent. So Tanika, please meet Sandeep da after the meeting and ask him for a list of ghazal artistes whose works, in his learned opinion, we should not mix. Please remember not to touch any of those, okay? What's next? A small coffee break, perhaps?'

During the coffee break, Solapurkar introduced Mrigo to Deepak Daga and the others in the team. 'A very bright young man. Perhaps, if we are lucky, he will bring his talent to our great company,' he said, embarrassing Mrigo greatly.

Mrigankomouli Bhattacharjee. Thirty-two. A bachelor. MBA from Harvard Business School. Coaxed into returning to work in India by his doting parents because they could not bear to be separated from their only child.

But this brief CV doesn't quite explain why he was in the Conference Corner of India Musica that morning. So let us go back a little.

Mrigo had had no wish to go to the US to study in the first place, because he had no desire to get an MBA degree. All he'd wanted was to be a musician, a sitar player, because he was reared by his parents to love and respect Hindustani classical music. Baba, his father, could play the surbahar, and had learnt from one of Annapurna Debi's disciples. Ma, his mother, was an expert in Atul Prasad songs. From the time he was only a toddler, Mrigo was taken along for every music festival and conference in Kolkata that his parents attended. They were delighted when they discovered that their little boy listened to classical music with rapt attention and was soon identifying raags as if he had them embedded in that curly little head of his. By the time he was five, they were certain he was gifted, and on the advice of Baba's guru, sent him for sitar lessons to Pandit Debendra

Datta, a follower of the Maihar-Senia gharana. Many of the current crop of promising sitar players were Deben Babu's disciples and they were all serious players with a solid understanding of technique and *raagdari*, not the circus acts that were becoming popular. Left to himself, Mrigo might have preferred to sing, but Ma felt that since Baba played the surbahar, his son should learn to play the sitar—which she called *shaytaar*, in her Bengali brogue. And that settled it.

Little Mrigo started learning the sitar, and in a few years even his reticent, difficult-to-please guru had to admit—never in the boy's presence, of course—that Mrigo's talent for music was '*awshaadhaaron*'. Everyone knew how impossibly miserly Deben Babu was when it came to expressing appreciation, so anyone rated 'extraordinary' by him was certain to be prodigiously talented.

Mind you, Mrigo was also a model student in school—one whose uniform was always spick and span, whose homework was always submitted on time; a topper in his class, with a beautiful, neat handwriting, who made a habit of winning scholar badges and prizes all the time. And of course he collected prizes and trophies at all the music and talent competitions for young musicians that were organized in Kolkata.

He was perfect, young Mrigo, and as he grew a little older, his brilliance in sitar-playing and academics seemed even to him to make up for the misfortune of large flat feet, a podgy figure that had blossomed man-boobs by the time he was fifteen, and the fact that he was a virtual marionette in the hands of his Ma and Baba. He was their obsession. They sat in stiff, restrained silence while he played on stage, but their hearts burst with pride when people applauded their Mrigo. Ma called him '*Shaytar Shomrat*', the Emperor of Sitar, and massaged his fingers every day; Baba called him 'Junior Robi Shonkor' and personally clipped his nails every week.

And yet, when he told his parents, at age eighteen, of his desire to be a full-time musician, he had his first ever full-blown argument with them. In fact, it wasn't an argument but them saying 'No!' repeatedly, with greater vehemence each time, and him asking 'But why?' repeatedly, until he found himself shouting at the top of his voice and Ma began to sob and beg Mother Durga to take her away. Ma had an attack of migraine that evening and was in bed for a week. Baba looked grim and moved around the house in hostile silence, not saying the words but clearly blaming Mrigo for pushing his mother to a premature death. Mrigo was miserable and bewildered—they loved classical music, and they had made *him* love it even more, so why were they reacting like this? The mystery was solved one afternoon when he heard Ma speaking to her brother on the phone. To make sure that her cruel and wayward son heard the conversation, she left her bed and came to sit at the dining table, just outside his room.

'Na Dada, amar shoreer ekdom bhalo nei (No, Dada, I'm not well at all),' she sniffled. 'I'm not well at all...Take care of myself? I shouldn't worry? Tell me how, Dada. Tell me, no—when our future is dark. All our hopes are shattered. Our own child...I carried him in my womb for nine-and-a-half months—nine-and-a-half months! And he shouts at me! Even at his God-like father! What is our crime, Dada? We went hungry to give him the best education...and now he is a genius by God's grace, is he not? Everyone...our entire clan has been waiting for him to make us proud. We have saved to send him to America—America, Dada, even *you* say that is where he should go to study further. Big companies will run after him, they will beg him to join them. Our old age will be golden, all our sacrifice...And now he says he'll become a *shaytar* master! *Bhogobaan!* He will starve...and what of our dreams, our reputation...No, Dada, I don't think I'll get well...Come and meet your little sister one last time, Dada...'

It was Mrigo who relented finally, after many weeks of Ma moaning and sighing and Baba glaring at him accusingly. 'Your Ma's migraine has made her blood pressure dangerously high,' Baba said to the TV screen one evening. He had stopped addressing Mrigo directly ever since the day of the argument. 'Doctor Chakladhar says she will develop a dangerous heart condition. You can have the pleasure of lighting her pyre very soon.' It was at this point that Mrigo's resolve collapsed and he finally agreed to make his way to Harvard for an MBA degree. He was sick of the melodrama.

Mrigo stayed in the US for almost four years, during which period he remained aloof and unrelenting towards his parents. Not once did he express even the slightest desire to return to India for an annual holiday, or even his favourite cousin's wedding. He had decided that his parents had banished him to America against his wishes and once banished, he had no desire to come back to them.

But Ma had her way again. This time she conned him into taking the fastest flight to Kolkata by faking a critical illness. And once he was with her, she threatened to kill herself if he so much as thought of going back to America. Unable to return to his life of freedom, far away from parental control, Mrigo slipped into deep depression. It happened gradually, until one day even Ma realized that the matter was serious. And she realized, too, that using her migraine or blood pressure as weapons would only make things worse. Instead, she became a dynamo in the kitchen, turning out Mrigo's favourite recipes almost by the hour. He barely pecked at them. His anxious father now racked his brains for a way to pull him out of depression. The best course, he concluded, was to find some job opportunity for Mrigo in India that would offer him a decent career and also keep him connected to the music he loved so passionately. And then he remembered Sandeep Solapurkar from India Musica.

Bhattacharjee senior had first met Solapurkar at a record collector's meet, and they had exchanged 78 rpm records of rare Hindustani classical tracks from each other's collections on several occasions. Locating Solapurkar's phone number in his handwritten diary, Bhattacharjee called and requested a meeting and confided in him about Mrigo's condition. And it was in response to Solapurkar's suggestion that Mrigo attend office with him for a few days to see if indeed the work interested him, that Mrigo found himself in the India Musica Conference Corner that morning, sipping coffee and trying not to giggle every time he saw Tanika Talwar and was reminded of 'guzzling'.

In about fifteen minutes, the meeting and discussions resumed, and this time it was Raghu M. who was asked to share his plans and ideas with the group. Raghu spoke with an air of nonchalance, a couldn't-care-less attitude that was in equal parts natural and cultivated.

'Look guys, forgive the informality, I'm not really used to this kind of formal shit,' he began. 'But I'm happy to join the team and all that. Now I'm pretty sure you guys would not have heard the indie bands and artistes I'm planning to bring on board, so I've made some arrangements to play you some of their tracks. I think you should know the kind of artistes and music you will be representing, so tell me if any of these would work for you. But before I go ahead, let me ask you something. India Musica is known for its very serious classical music or its very serious money-making music from Hindi films and stuff like that. So do you guys now want to make a tentative initial investment in the indie music scene, or would you like to go the whole hog?'

Daga said, 'For this presentation let's go the whole hog and then we can decide whether we should perhaps support something more mass-oriented or closer to popular film music.'

'Okay then,' responded Raghu, 'fasten your seat belts and here we go! So there's this all-girl band that I've been following for a while and I think we should look at signing them because I feel they have star potential. They're all hot looking chicks, by the way. I know this isn't PC but screw it. Truth is, looks matter. So, to repeat—these chicks are serious eye candy.'

'How many?' asked Mukherji suddenly.

'Five of 'em, man,' said Raghu, as if this were a magic number. 'And all twenty something.'

Mukherji conscientiously took down notes, even though he had an assistant scribbling furiously behind him.

Raghu continued hard-selling the girl band: 'So the kind of music they make is very modern but they have several Indian influences too. One of them is trained in classical and she's always dressed in a sari-shari. She also dances when she performs and lets her knee-length hair fly in the air as she swings and twirls while singing. Sometimes she plays a guitar, and for some tracks she uses an ektara, Baul-style. But boy, what a performer she is! Solid! So she's the lead singer and then there are these four other babes in the band.'

'What's the band called?' asked Daga.

'Oh sorry, I should have told you in the first place. Well, they call themselves The Badass Bandariyas.'

Mrigo snorted. The lady assistant sitting next to him said '*Eesh*' under her breath and tittered into her printed handkerchief. At the high table, Mukherji leaned forward earnestly and asked, 'Sorry, Mr Roghu, I could not hear. Please could you repeat the name?'

'Sure, they're called The Badass Bandariyas.'

'Err,' interjected Solapurkar in his very superior and very genteel manner. 'Is this supposed to be some sort of joke? Because if it is, I'm afraid it is in very poor taste.'

'No, Mr Solapurkar, this isn't a joke,' Raghu M. said

testily. 'The girls call themselves Badass Bandariyas. Can we hear their music before you object to anything else? May I proceed?'

Daga intervened. 'No interruptions, please. Go ahead, Raghu.'

Not encountering any further objections, Raghu proceeded to play a video on the wall-mounted screen.

The track started with a pitch-black screen, and the sound of what appeared to be a strong breeze blowing on location, and the tinkling of wind chimes. The dense black dissolved into light to the sound of heavy breathing, to reveal a young woman in ushtraasana, the camel pose, with an enormous eye painted in the middle of her forehead. She was dressed in dramatic yellow and red robes, her flowing tresses were worn loose and swept the floor, and her eyes were painted like a Kathakali dancer's. Around her were ranged four other band members, also in colourful robes, but their faces were covered with huge Chhau-style masks. One of them had an electric guitar strapped across her body and another a bass guitar, the third stood ready to pound the drums before her, and the fourth, the tallest, loomed large behind a keyboard. Each of the instruments had been painted and decorated in fluorescent, glittering colours.

The four masked women began to twirl around slowly, gently waving their outstretched arms up and down to the sound of the breeze and the chimes, while the yogini in ushtraasana merely moved her pupils from side to side, the whites of her eyes shining wildly. Suddenly, to the crash of cymbals, the yogini stood up straight, raised her arms to the sky and rent the air with a deafening scream as she leapt up high, screeching 'Aaaaaaaayeeeeeee!' As she landed back on earth to another crash of cymbals, the drummer started playing a simple four-beat groove. The guitar, bass and keyboard joined in, as the yogini struck feral poses at each beat, flashing her eyes and dancing some kind of war dance. A few bars later, four girls in Chhau masks began to sing over and over again in a menacing growl:

Ga ga ga ga gaga re sa
1 2 3 4 1 2 3 4

The lead singer, the yogini, then broke into an extension of the 'ga ga re sa' theme, singing at breakneck speed:

Gugraysa Gugraysa
Gugmapa Gugmapa
Pupnisa Pupnisa
Gaaaaaaa ga gaaaaaaa

The stunningly off-tune chant was repeated by the band over and over, while the lead singer hollered in the gaps:

(Chorus) Gugraysa (Lead) Got it!
(Chorus) Gugmapa (Lead) I Got it!
(Chorus) Gugmapa (Lead) Flaunt it!
(Chorus) Pupnisa (Lead) I'll flaunt it!

Over the extended 'Gaaaaaaa ga gaaaaaaa' the lead singer screamed, 'Aaaaaayeeeeeeee!'

And then came the lyrics:

Roko nahin mujhe toko nahin, main hoon Badass Bandariya
Jo roka mujhe to mein chheenoongi, jhaptoongi, kaatoongi, peetoongi yaaaaaa,
Main hoon, main hoon
Main hoon, main hoon
Badass bandariyaaaaa
Bad
Ass
Bandariyaaaaaa

(Don't you stop me, don't you nag me, I'm a badass she-monkey
Stop me and I'll snatch, I'll scratch
I'll bite, I'll beat yaaaaaa
I am, I am
I am, yes I am
A badass she-monkey

Bad
Ass
Bandariyaaaaaa)

At this juncture, Solapurkar pushed his chair back, rose with as much dignity as he could muster in his rage, and walked out of the room. Daga glanced at his personal assistant, indicating that he should follow Solapurkar.

Raghu M. paused the music video with a smug smile on his face and asked, 'Too much for you guys or should we carry on?'

No one seemed to be in a hurry to respond, each waiting for someone else to speak first. Tanika jumped in readily and declared: 'I think these girls are *awesome*! Pretty much superstar material—and in a reely contemporary way. I mean, their stuff is good—like, good enough for the international market. I'd like to see them at Midem perhaps, in the India Musica pavilion. They'll be a rage! Like...'

It was at this rather inopportune moment, as Tanika was in raptures and Raghu M. was punching the air above him in triumph, that Daga's assistant escorted Solapurkar back into the room to join the meeting. As he settled into his chair, the crease on his forehead became deeper on hearing Tanika repeat her suggestion that India Musica should take The Badass Bandariyas to a prestigious music business event like Midem.

'Mr Mukherji,' he began, 'I'd like your permission to put forth my point of view.'

'Oh of course, Sandeep da,' said Mr Mukherji hurriedly, and Solapurkar took a deep breath before he said, 'Mr Daga, I know you have asked me to be patient with our young colleagues. But this is getting to be unbearable for me. I have been part of your Artiste and Repertoire team for decades, Mr Daga, and therefore it is with considerable experience that I speak. We are a music company and not a circus. Promoting an act like this... this—well, quite silly Bandariya act—is going to turn us into a third-grade circus company and nothing more. These girls are downright *besura*, absolutely out of tune. Can we not hear that? Have we lost our sense of hearing? I realize I am going against your instructions, Mr Daga, but it is impossible for me to not speak my mind about this nonsense. If this is the kind of music you want to promote, I would, with regret, be forced to leave.'

'No, no Sandeep da, please don't say such things,' implored Mr Mukherji, but before he could soothe Solapurkar's badly ruffled feathers, Raghu M. was up in arms: 'This is so unfair. It's unbelievable! If you're going to let him get away with such rude remarks about the music I'd like to promote, why hire me in the first place? I don't understand his obsession with classical, but I don't go around saying it isn't any good.' At this point he looked straight at Solapurkar and said, 'Do I, *haan*?'

Solapurkar rallied: 'You can't say it isn't good, Mr Raghu M., because the music I have recorded for this company *is* good. It is *excellent*. And I can get away with all manner of rude remarks about the music your Bandariyas produce because it simply doesn't deserve to be called music. It is noise and it is terrible even as noise.'

Raghu was now livid. He leaned forward menacingly and hollered, '*Fuck* you, you piece of horse-shit! A tight-assed old bandicoot, that's what you are.'

An uproar ensued and several at the table rose to their feet.

'Take back your words, take back your words right now, you impudent, insolent boy!' yelled Solapurkar, rising from his chair.

'Gentlemen!' said Daga, but for once no one was listening to him.

Mrigo looked around in horror, and decided he had had enough. Taking advantage of the mayhem and noise in the room, he slipped out, making sure he took his bag and other belongings with him because he had no intention of ever returning to the madhouse.

He reached his home fairly late that evening, just as his parents were getting ready for dinner. He did not offer them any explanation about why he was late, or tell them about his day at India Musica. Already rattled by his condition over the last couple of months, they decided to let him be; he would probably treat their questions as an intrusion. But once dinner was over, and the three of them prepared to retire to their respective rooms, Mrigo said to them:

'I start work tomorrow morning as marketing head at Prima. They make sports shoes and gear. They have absolutely nothing to do with music. That's why I decided to join them. And that's all I'd like to tell you.'

He turned and left. Baba made to go after him but Ma stopped him with the tiniest shake of her head.

'Don't ask him anything today,' she said. 'And I have heard of Prima, Dada's friend worked there. It's a good company. MNC. I hope they give him a car and a driver...'

Manzoor Rehmati

Manzoor Ahmad 'Rehmati' stood on the pavement opposite one of the many mansions dotting the upmarket South Delhi locality he was visiting. He was dressed in a white silk kurta-pyjama that he had saved for just such an occasion, and shiny white faux leather sandals. The sandals were such a tight squeeze for his swollen feet—a condition that had troubled him for over a year now—that his heels jutted out over the back of the sandals, and the little toes on each of his feet sprang out disobediently from the front strap. But for that small imperfection, he was quite pleased with his appearance. He had even doused himself generously with a not too cheap imitation of Lucknow's most popular brand of rose *ittar*. As he lifted a hand with henna stained nails to pat his oily hair into place, an array of silver and gold rings with bulbous, coloured stones gleamed in the late-morning sun. He looked somewhat disreputable, not the kind of man you might want to invite home for tea; but this wasn't an opinion Manzoor had of himself. He was, as we have noted, pleased with his appearance; and he was very hopeful of making a favourable impression at the meeting he was heading into. The three bags he was carrying—two over his right shoulder, the long straps tucked into his armpit, and one in his left hand—contained all the vital ingredients for the successful completion of his mission.

Manzoor was eager and ready for action. He stepped off the pavement, crossed over to the other side of the road, and walked purposefully to the imposing gate that barred entry into the particular mansion that was his destination. Here, his brief wave of confidence subsided. He looked around in slight confusion, trying to locate the switch for a bell that would announce his arrival, but found none. Unsure of what to do, he stood still for a few seconds, until a strong sense of being watched made him look to his right. He noticed a narrow wooden cabin, from which a security guard seated on a high stool was staring at him in hostile silence. Both men stared confrontationally at each other for several moments. Then Manzoor decided to break the deadlock and asked hesitantly, '*Sahab ghar par hain?* (Is sahab at home?)'

Emboldened by the hesitation in Manzoor's voice, the guard asked with a curl of the lip: '*Sahab? Kaun se sahab? Iss kothi mein do sahib hain. Kaun se sahab se milna hai tumhein?* (Which sahab? There are two sahabs in this bungalow. Which one do you want to meet?)'

Manzoor replied: 'It is Bade Khan sahab who has asked me to come and meet him today. May I go in?'

'*Yaheen ruko* (Wait right here),' snapped the guard and turned his back on Manzoor and disappeared into the house. It was some ten minutes before he returned, by which time sweat thick with jasmine hair oil had begun to drip down Manzoor's forehead. The surly guard finally opened one half of the gate and let Manzoor in grudgingly.

'You can come in. Wait in the lobby till sahab sends someone for you.'

'*Ji*, guard sahab, as you say,' said Manzoor ingratiatingly, not wanting his mission to be sabotaged by someone as insignificant as a security guard. Mopping his brow with a flowered hand towel, he walked in.

The lobby was a sort of bare bones waiting area. The two armless plastic Nilkamal chairs set against one wall, with a table between them, were clearly meant to put the bums resting on them in their proper hierarchical place, several rungs below the residents of the house. The lobby itself—a side room, in fact—was small and a little stuffy. But Manzoor told himself that all this was inconsequential compared to the importance of his mission. He would grin and bear it. Besides, he had sat in tinier rooms and on far more uncomfortable chairs.

Setting down his bags, he waited patiently, occasionally clearing his throat noisily in the hope that the sahab and memsahab would become aware of his presence if they were anywhere in the vicinity. But to no avail.

It was a good fifteen minutes before a maid in a blindingly blue cotton sari entered the waiting area holding a small tray with a glass of water on it. She thrust the water at him sullenly and asked if he wanted tea, her tone indicating that she would prefer an answer in the negative. Manzoor told himself she did not know any better, lowly creature that she was. What had her wretched world to do with his? How could she know that he was one of the most popular harmonium players in the capital city? No, it would be too much to expect this poor, illiterate servant to know that he was an ustad.

'Make me some tea with lots of milk and plenty of sugar,' he said a little imperiously. '*Aur suno, kuchh biscoot bhi leti aana.* (And listen, get me some biscuits, too.)'

To this command the maid responded with a silent, sharp look of such disdain that Manzoor dropped his gaze to the floor. Obstinate wench, he thought to himself as she turned and left. He waited for her to return with his cup of tea. Ten minutes passed, then fifteen, but there was no sign of either the maid or the residents of the mansion. Impatient, Manzoor began playing an imaginary harmonium on his knee, making strange jerky movements with his left hand, while the fingers of his right hand danced in the air. So engrossed was he, his eyes closed and head bobbing, that he did not notice the maid finally returning with his sweet and milky tea, until she let out a high-pitched giggle. Manzoor opened his eyes and smiled sheepishly. Then he leaned forward to take the cup and saucer from the maid, slyly touching her hand in the process. She continued to giggle and ran out of the room, almost doubling over with laughter. He called out to remind her of the biscuits when suddenly the lady of the house swished elegantly into the room.

Manzoor snapped to attention, hastily putting down his cup and saucer. He shot out of the flimsy chair, bent forward from the waist and, lifting his hand to his forehead repeatedly, delivered an exaggerated salaam. Having completed the obeisance, he said, '*Khala*, bless me, please.' Straightening up just a little, he folded his hands in supplication, and stared at her adoringly. '*Buss aap hi ki nazr-e-karam bachaa sakti hai iss badnaseeb ko. Rahem karein mujh par!* (Only your blessings can save this unfortunate creature. Have mercy on me!)'

Richly attired in an expensive silk sari, and coiffed, bejewelled and sparkling, the lady of the house, Begum Shagufta Khan, accepted Manzoor's homage, waving a hand over his head in blessing, but making sure it did not come in contact with his greasy hair. '*Khush raho*,' she said. 'Come, Khan-sahab has been waiting for you, but I couldn't call for you earlier because there has been such a crowd of people around him that I barely got a minute to inform him that you are here.'

She turned briskly, with surprising grace given her age and girth, and Manzoor followed, hurriedly scooping up his three bags. She spoke without pause as they walked down a short corridor. 'I'm happy you are on time. So many people beg Khan-sahab for an appointment and then make him wait when he gives them one. I hate it. It really makes me angry. But you are a good fellow, your elders have taught you good manners. But they must all be dead now, no? Your *waalid* I know about, of course, poor man. How many years has it been? But he was very old, wasn't he? *Chalo, jo khuda ko manzoor* (Whatever be God's will.) *Achha,* how are your boys? Doing well? How many?'

Before Manzoor could reply, she said, '*Achha,* now you must keep your request short. I know how much you like to talk, you talk too much. I don't mind that, but Khan-sahab is different, as you know. And he's busy, his mind is always busy...So not too much, okay?'

She stopped at the open door of a room and signalled to Manzoor that he should remove his footwear before he entered. Glad of the opportunity to relieve his feet of the painful sandals, Manzoor complied happily and followed her into the stately room where sat the master of the house, on a raised wooden stage-like platform covered with an exquisite Persian carpet.

Khan-sahab cut a fine figure. A handsome man in his sixties, he was always immaculately, expensively dressed. The *chikankaari* on his spotless white kurta could only have been the work of the finest *kaarigars* in the country, and his diamond-studded kurta buttons were brilliant but not flashy. A fine grey cashmere scarf was casually draped over one shoulder, and matched his casually tousled salt-and-pepper locks. The gold ring on his left hand had a 'pigeon-blood' ruby set in it, and on the little finger of his right hand he wore a large turquoise set in silver, probably a gift from a pir, a spiritual master. He looked royal, imposing and utterly convinced of his nobility as he sat regally in what could only be called a modern-day durbar. Poor Manzoor looked like a court jester in comparison, and he knew it. But it was a small matter—if being a court jester was what it took to accomplish his mission, he did not mind being one.

Khan-sahab, or Ustad Riwayat Ali Khan, renowned vocalist with awards galore, reigned supreme in the world of Hindustani classical music. Not only was he one of the country's most highly decorated and star musicians, he also had considerable influence in political circles, having learnt very early in his career that an artiste desirous of popular and abiding success should never have political opinions, and should cultivate the powerful no matter which political party or business empire they belonged to. His name often topped the list of patrons, advisors and members of governing bodies of almost all noteworthy committees related to art and culture in the country. Any artiste whom he decided to recommend for an award invariably received it. His record for the prestigious Padma Shri and Padma Bhushan awards was particularly impressive. In the last decade, six people he had nominated had found their names on the list of Padma awardees released by the government of India on the eve of Republic Day every year. Merit seemed not to matter when weighed against the Ustad's recommendation. You could be a dolt and still get a Padma award if the Ustad wanted you to get it. And if he so much as raised an eyebrow or frowned a little when an artiste's name was mentioned in the selection committee, the Padma slipped out of the hapless artiste's fingers, however meritorious he or she may be. No one in the classical music and dance world had the gumption to say it openly, but a lot of sniggering accompanied the gossip that Khan-sahab's benevolence was responsible for the Padmas that had been bestowed on a raucous and off-key vocalist who had managed to curry favour with him (though no one seemed to know exactly how) and a wealthy socialite turned dancer with no sense of rhythm, of whom the Ustad had grown extremely fond.

Manzoor desperately wanted a Padma award, and had realized that the only way he could get one was if someone as powerful as Khan-sahab turned magnanimous and recommended his name for it. Otherwise, a mere unlettered accompanist like him would be ignored. All he needed was an audience with the great man—he had met him before, of course, not once but several times; he had been an accompanist at quite a few of Khan-sahab's concerts. But he needed at least a half-hour one-on-one meeting, and perhaps three or four such sessions, in order to explain to Khan-sahab why he deserved his generosity; why he was a good candidate for a Padma Shri. And after he discovered that Khan-sahab's mother-in-law, his begum's late mother, had been born and raised in Shahabad, Manzoor's own hometown, Manzoor decided that Begum sahiba was his only hope. He had begun to seek her out at every concert of Khan-sahab's in Delhi and soon won her interest, perhaps even affection, because of the Shahabad connection. It helped that she liked to talk and warmed to anyone who listened to her in silence, only exclaiming occasionally when she praised her husband, her son—their *sahabzada,* 'already a genius vocalist'—her married daughter, her own parents and, in a roundabout manner, herself (how, for instance, Khan-sahab trusted no one but her with the washing of his clothes). Manzoor was very good at this. It also helped that the begum liked to have her voluminous handbag and her cell phone carried for her. Manzoor taught himself to be very good at this, too. He took to addressing her as '*Khala*', mother's sister, bowing low in an exaggerated salaam, before taking charge of her handbag and cell phone.

Always street smart, Manzoor had learnt several valuable lessons when he migrated from Shahabad, in Hardoi district of Uttar Pradesh, to Delhi, where he had heard artistes were paid five times more for concerts than the meagre amounts he received in Shahabad and other towns of Hardoi. It turned out that Manzoor had, unwittingly, chosen the right time to make the shift to Delhi; there was a dearth of harmonium players in the city who were good enough to provide accompaniment to classical music. The few who were half-way decent preferred ghazal and bhajan concerts, where they earned more. Manzoor made himself available to every classical vocalist in need of a harmonium player, demanding not much more than his Hardoi rates in the beginning. He also added 'Rehmati' to his name; a distinctive, poetic name that spoke of his humility and good taste, besides being easy to remember.

Soon he became the only harmonium player to be booked for almost any major classical music event or festival in Delhi. His rate and total earnings went up, and he was able to send money back to Shahabad every month, squirrelling away whatever he could to improve the two-room semi-pukka hut that his family lived in. As Manzoor prospered in Delhi, the hut metamorphosed into a three-storey brick and mortar house painted in loud blues and greens. It was the envy of all the other musicians in Shahabad whose lives continued to be wretched.

Manzoor continued to forge ahead in Delhi, acquiring some money, if not wealth—enough to buy a one-room-kitchen flat in one of the narrowest by-lanes of Old Delhi, where, some years later, he would ask his teenage sons to join him. He also acquired a fierce love for liquor, usually the *tharra, narangi* or *santari* varieties of country liquor, and an intense yearning for a Padma award. He pursued both obsessions with remarkable doggedness. His love for liquor soon landed him with severe diabetes—and its attendant problems like poor eyesight. While his other obsession, the lust for a Padma award, turned him into an avid collector of virtually any item or object that could prove he was worthy of the award.

Armed with this entire collection, carefully packed in the three bags that he had brought with him, Manzoor waited eagerly to convince Khan-sahab that he, Manzoor Ahmad Rehmati of Shahabad, the favourite harmonium accompanist of every major classical singer living in or visiting Delhi, the most powerful of all the cities of Hindustan, richly deserved the Padma Shri award. The largest bag contained a huge collection of LP records, cassettes, CDs, VCDs and DVDs of concerts at which he had accompanied every contemporary Hindustani vocalist worth his or her name. He would have liked to have at least one solo album in the collection, but alas, no record label had agreed—it was an old prejudice; the harmonium had never been accorded any real respect in the classical world. Never mind, Manzoor consoled himself. Once he got the Padma, they would all run after him, and then he would pick and choose.

The other two bags Manzoor had brought along contained a gigantic photo album each. Of these, the album with a plastic cover of fluorescent blue sprayed with tiny pink flowers carried no photographs at all. It contained instead a fat wad of slip covers inside each of which was enshrined a letter of recommendation from a musician, a minor politician, a film star, a senior bureaucrat, a university professor—anyone who was or appeared important in some degree—declaring Manzoor worthy of a Padma award. There was a story Manzoor could tell about how he had obtained each of these letters of recommendation: months of bowing and scraping before the private assistants and henchmen of MPs and MLAs, often parting with some of his hard-earned money; writing hundreds of fan letters to film stars; stalking celebrities, however minor, at music concerts, book launches, crafts melas or food festivals until they relented and sent him a letter of recommendation. The trick was to spot a celebrity who looked kind or gullible, or past his or her prime and in great need of attention and flattery, and, more important, to have no shame or self-respect and chase people without fear of being humiliated. Some of the vocalists whose recommendations he had received had been dastardly enough to give him the letter he wanted but conveniently forgot to pay him for three or four concerts. Manzoor had put up with the deceit—it was a small price to pay for a Padma award; but some day he would shame them publicly.

The other mammoth album with a shiny green cover contained a slew of press cuttings and photographs of Manzoor with important personalities. Behind each photograph was inscribed a caption written by one of Manzoor's sons: 'Papa with President of India', 'Papa ji with Great Film Star Urmila Thakur ji', and so on. In some of the photographs, 'Papa' and 'Papa ji' had been scratched out and replaced with 'Ustad Manzoor Ahmad Rehmati Shahabadi'. The hand here was a bit unsteady, but it did not appear to be a young person's hand. More likely, it was the hand of someone who wrote under the influence—of anger or passion or drink, or all three.

Manzoor now set down his bounty before Khan-sahab, squatted on his haunches behind the bags, and stated his case.

'*Huzoor*, you have known me for years, and I have been lucky to have accompanied you on so many occasions. You remember that concert in Gwalior, when you sang Darbari? *Mash-a-Allah!* What a Darbari that was! You sang for four hours non-stop and even then the audience refused to let you go. There have been so many memorable concerts that generations will remember, and this *naacheez*, this nobody, has had the great good fortune of accompanying you and witnessing your magic. So you know my work, Khan-sahab, and my loyalty to you. If you were to recommend my name for a Padma award, *Huzoor*, my life's mission would be accomplished. My beloved Shahabad could tell the world that even a Shahabadi has received a Padma award, and all because of the magnanimity of a divine musician. One nod from you, Khan-sahab, and this dream would become a reality for me.' At this point Manzoor solicitously pressed the Ustad's feet, then continued, 'Look, *Huzoor*, I have collected all the material required to recommend my name.'

He hastily unzipped the bags, and laid out the albums and CDs and cassettes before Khan-sahab. Browsing through the albums and sifting indifferently through the albums, Khan-sahab occasionally stifled a yawn, grunted approvingly now and again, and chuckled sarcastically at times. Finally, he waved a hand dismissively and said to Manzoor. '*Achha, yaar,* let me see what I can do. Don't worry about it, Manzoor *mian*. If Allah wants you to get the Padma Shri, you will get it. In the meantime, let's talk music. Do you remember, your *waalid marhoom* Zahoor Ahmad had a collection of rare compositions in some very unusual raags? What was that Shreetank *bandish*? Or did he call it Tankashree? I have never heard it from anyone else. Do you remember it?'

It did not take Manzoor even a second to gather what Khan-sahab was getting at. He did some quick thinking and made his move. If giving the *bandish* to Khan-sahab meant a Padma coming his way, it would be an investment worth the barter. In his mind, he quickly asked his dear departed father's forgiveness, flashed a toothy smile at Khan-sahab, and said: 'Tankashree? Of course, *Huzoor*. What would I do with that *bandish*? It will find a worthy place in your collection, Ustad ji. Here is how my *waalid sahab* would sing it...'

Just as he was about to burst into song, Riwayat Ali Khan raised an imperious hand and said, 'No, no, not like this. *Mian*, these are rare pieces, not to be given and taken in jest. Come back next week and we will do a recording session right here, in this room. And then you record the Tankashree *cheez* for me, as well as any other rare compositions you feel I should have. And don't be a *kanjoos, mian*! You play the harmonium, you don't sing, so don't be a dog in the manger and take them to the grave with you. Give them to a good *gavaiyya*, and when I or my *sahabzada* sing any of these, we will tell the world that we got these from the family of Zahoor Ahmad Shahabadi, no less. Understood?'

Manzoor would have liked to wrap up the deal then and there. He did not want to waste any more time, but he had no option but to shake his head obediently, even enthusiastically. 'You are right as always, Khan-sahab. These compositions are lost treasures in my care. Once you sing them, the world will know their true worth and will also respect my father, may Allah bless his soul, for his wisdom and knowledge.'

In a few minutes, he had been dismissed for the day and found himself lugging his three bags back to his modest home in Old Delhi. For the next three months or so, Manzoor was summoned repeatedly by Khan-sahab for almost eight to ten recording sessions. He ended up recording for Khan-sahab forty-five compositions in the rarest of raags from his late father's hitherto secret collection. Khan-sahab would often receive phone calls during the recording sessions, stroll out of the room to answer his calls and then return only after an hour or so to terminate the session abruptly, saying he had some urgent work to attend to. Manzoor wondered sometimes whether he was entertaining other guests and supplicants for Padma awards in his magnificent living room while he made Manzoor give up his family's musical treasures. As the days dragged on, he became more and more restless and frustrated because not once during the recording sessions did Khan-sahab give even the slightest hint of his intentions regarding a Padma award for Manzoor.

In desperation, Manzoor turned to his other obsession, liquor. He would drink every night, and become aggressive and violent if his sons, both budding musicians, tried to keep him away from the bottle. Soon, he was drinking during the day as well, and could barely conceal the strong whiff of stale liquor on his breath when he went to Khan-sahab's home for the recording sessions. One afternoon Khan-sahab dismissed him within ten minutes of the recording having begun, and told him to come back a week later. When Manzoor turned up that day, a little unsteady on his feet, the unfriendly guard at the gate glared at him with more disgust than hostility, went inside the house, probably reported Manzoor's inebriated state to the sahab and memsahab, and returned to inform Manzoor that there would be no session today as Khan-sahab had to go out on urgent work. Cursing under his breath, Manzoor lurched away from the gate, and felt his head spinning as he turned. It was a hot day. He felt incredibly thirsty and reached inside his bag for the quarter bottle he had stashed away. As soon as he was able to flag down an auto rickshaw and stumble into it, he put the bottle to his mouth and took a swig. As the driver lurched and braked repeatedly on his way to Old Delhi, Manzoor experienced repeated bouts of breathlessness. By the time he reached the road which led to the *gali* where he lived, he was feeling nauseous. As he staggered towards his home, retching and gasping intermittently, some neighbours recognized him and tried to help. But with a sudden, last gasp, he collapsed on the road, a few metres from his home. A crowd gathered around him, while some boys ran to his home calling out to his sons. Naved and Zubaid, his two sons, rushed out towards him, and carried him home, yelling for an ambulance and crying for help.

Manzoor could not hear them. He had slipped into a coma. He died late that night, and his distraught sons took his body back to Shahabad to bury him in the same graveyard where his father and grandfather lay. Some weeks later, Ustad Riwayat Ali Khan recorded Tankashree and other rare raags for his next album, but he forgot to acknowledge Manzoor's father. Months passed, summer turned to winter, and on 25th January in the new year, the Padma awards were announced. Manzoor Ahmad Sahahabadi's name did not feature in the list of awardees.

The Man Who Made Stars

The episode was over and done with, but Manjusha's face was still flushed with indignation and outrage. As she sat down at the small and by-now rickety table inherited from her grandfather's library, and poured herself a glass of water, she could think of at least a dozen sharp and stinging retorts she could have included in the tongue lashing she had just delivered to the man on the phone. She wondered for a moment whether she should call him back and pelt him once again with the many sallies buzzing around in her head now, but decided against it. Enough, she said to herself. The toad might just see it as some kind of victory—that she was relenting, that she was only pretending to be appalled and furious all over again, when in fact she was only preparing to apologize.

Really, the stupid, smug fool had sounded just like the sort of man who would think that. His pride wouldn't allow him to believe that he could be refused, in bed or in business. The world was full of such men. 'Toad, big fat toad who forgot to grow up,' she said to herself and began to giggle. Now that her outrage was fading, she even found it laughable.

It had all started with the telephone next to her bed ringing stridently that afternoon just as she was about to drift into a nap. Contented and at peace after a hearty meal and the rigorous, punishing *riyaaz* session that had preceded it, she was still singing phrases and clusters of Raag Yamani Bilawal in her head. New phrases and patterns from the same raag usually continued to sprout abundantly in the back of her mind long after she finished her daily practice sessions. This had always been the case, ever since she took to music as a young girl. And little else had mattered after that.

Forty and single, Manjusha Saxena had found in music all the companionship she could have asked for and had committed herself to a lifelong pursuit of Hindustani classical music. Her father, the late Dhanya Kumar Saxena, had worked as a music teacher at one of the most prestigious public schools in the country and had ensured that his daughter was trained in music by a great scholar-guru of Gwalior. His efforts were suitably rewarded when Manjusha's talent and training soon positioned her among the most promising young musicians in Hindustani music circles. As she blossomed into a poised, talented and confident young artiste, Saxena sahab and his wife made a few feeble attempts to find a suitable spouse for the apple of their eyes. However, she brushed aside any suggestions in this regard, maintaining steadfastly that she had no desire to be saddled with a spouse lest he try and curb her independence and her commitment to music. After all, she had seen what had become of Mala, Shikha and Rashmi, her *guru-behens* who also came for *taaleem* to her guru. Each one had a fine voice, and all of them could have had flourishing careers as professional singers, but their guardians had wanted to settle them in holy matrimony. Soon, the three had all but abandoned music to dutifully look after home and hearth. Of course, she had no right to be critical of their choices, but she could not help noticing how wistful Mala had seemed when she met Manjusha at a recent concert in Ambala. She had congratulated Manjusha on a fine concert, but as she hugged Manjusha and bid her goodbye, she had said rather ruefully, 'I'm so proud of you, Manju. At least you were able to achieve what I wanted to but never could. You know how it is, looking after husband, in-laws and children. *Chalo*, I guess this was my destiny. Anyway, let's meet whenever you come next, okay?' It had broken Manjusha's heart, even as she had thought: But for the grace of God, that could have been me...

Once Saxena sahab breathed his last after a vicious

attack of dengue, Manjusha's mother too surrendered any dreams she may have nursed of finding a suitable partner for her daughter. Potential marital hurdles out of the way, Manjusha had speedily earned the reputation of being a brilliant performer with high standards of commitment and professionalism, and received a steady stream of invitations to perform at all the most prestigious music events and festivals in the country and overseas. She had also been singing on radio and later on television for close to three decades, and had recorded many successful albums. She was, for all purposes, something of a star in the Hindustani classical music circuit.

So when the phone rang that day, jolting her out of the beginnings of a gentle, sweet surrender to an afternoon nap, she had thought the call would probably be from an event organizer, asking about her availability to perform at yet another festival or the *punya tithi*, death anniversary, of some eminent musician. And if it was the latter, she would, doubtless, hear the perennial whine about the lack of event sponsors and funds, and she would listen and she would cluck in agreement and finally end up performing for virtually nothing—because to pay homage to an elder was the honourable thing to do. Naturally, then, she was totally unprepared for the conversation that was to follow, as she stretched across the bed to answer the phone and murmured a sleepy, mellow 'Hello?' In response, a fervent

Mata ki aarti, a particularly cacophonous ode to the Devi, played on the PBX board. Bells and conch shells pealed and crashed into her ear—anything in the name of the gods; she knew this well, and had realized it was futile to object. Frowning a little, she waited for someone to respond, but soon found herself listening intently to the *aarti.* Just when she was beginning to make her peace with the near complete disregard for harmony that the *aarti* displayed, a reedy-voiced female interjected and informed 'Madam Manjoo Shah' that 'Mister Raj Ramani of RR Film and Arts' would like to speak to her. Before Manjusha could reply, she was on hold again, and this time a chorus enthusiastically belting out '*Jai Mata di, Jai Mata di*', replete with frenzied manjiras and conch-shells, kept her company. Finally, a deep male voice with a strong Punjabi accent emerged from the ear piece:

'Hullo? Manjusha ji? Myself Raj Ramani. *Mein filmein banata hoon ji.* I make films. And I am a big fan of your singing, Manjusha ji, big fan! Madam, your classical of course—that is great, but personally I am a very great fan of your folk music. Hello? Hello? Manjusha ji?'

Manjusha was listening intently but in complete bewilderment as she tried to place the caller and get a sense of where this conversation was leading to. Was she hallucinating? Could this phone call be for real, or was it one of her mischievous friends trying to pull her leg?

Wasn't Raj Ramani the name of the director who had made the mega-hit multi-starrer *Yaara Dildara* a year ago? She remembered that he was among the many film-folk who had, on the advice of numerologists, altered the spelling of their names. Raj Ramani was now Raaj Rammaannii in print. But if indeed it was the celebrity Bollywood film-maker himself, what on earth could he want from her? And what in Heaven's name had given him the idea that she sang folk music?

In her confusion, she decided she had best disconnect the phone to buy some time, collect her wits and thoughts, and wait for the guy to call back if he really wanted to speak to her.

She was wide awake by then, and sat up in bed, mulling over the call, thinking of ways and means to confirm that it was indeed Ramani who had called and not some imposter. Within minutes, the phone rang again and the reedy-voiced receptionist was steering her back to the conversation with Ramani but only after a few hearty cheers of '*Jai Mata di*'. Manjusha told herself that this couldn't be a practical joke by one of her friends, and in order not to appear rude, she said cautiously, 'Mr Ramani? I'm so sorry, the phone got disconnected. And I don't use a cell phone at home so I didn't have your number to call back.'

'No problem, Manjusha ji. It happens,' Ramani said

blithely, not in the least cut up. 'My secretary is telling me you are not easy to contact on phone—you keep your mobile switched off most times. Only landline. I understand, ji. Artists are not like *aira gaira* people. They are very special. I am also like that. So you see, we will work very well together. Actually, I am working on my new film—*Dil Pardesi*.' He then began to list the many and great virtues of the film, all of which seemed to be over-the-top commercial. Manjusha punctuated Ramani's monologue with an occasional 'ji' to indicate that she was listening. Ramani continued enthusiastically, 'It is a total family drama, Manjusha ji, and all about Indian culture. Love story with *sanskar*—it is reflecting today's youth who are very modern but also have great respect for our tradition. Young people going for love marriage only with full blessings of their elders. Mini skirt and *mangalsutra*; women drinking wine-shine but keeping full *karva chauth* fast, not even water. You understand? I want to show that our original culture is great and it is also trendy. This is why I need your help. You see, your album of wedding songs is just super, in fact super-duper. In the full film, I want those wedding songs of yours. It will really suit the film, and your voice will be there throughout, from opening credit to closing credit.'

It dawned on Manjusha that Ramani was interested in the wedding songs from North India that she had recorded in a four-album set some years ago for a prominent music label. But if he wanted that album, she asked herself, why would he call her? His office could easily have obtained a licence from the music company or from IPRS. She liked to follow procedure, a habit she had inherited from her school-teacher father.

'Thank you so much, Mr Ramani, I'm so glad you enjoyed the album,' she said. 'Were you thinking of using any of the songs from those albums in your film? If so, you'll need to contact the music company, because they have the rights for the sound recording, or maybe IPRS does. I don't really know how this works.'

'What ji? Music company? IPRS? What is this IPRS?'

'Indian Performing Rights Society, Mr Ramani. It handles copyright matters for artistes who are its members.'

There was a brief silence. Raj Ramani was used to people approaching him for acting and singing breaks, and to his mind, he was doing Manjusha a big favour by inviting her to sing for him. He had fully expected Manjusha to be overjoyed and demonstrate that amply through her response. He certainly hadn't expected this practical, matter-of-fact statement about copyright, of all things! But he wasn't going to admit that he was shocked. The most he would show was puzzlement. He, too, was an artist, after all. He was above such mundane matters.

'*Hain ji?*' he said. 'Copyright? Oh, don't worry about

copyright-shopyright. My office will handle that. I don't understand these things. But tell me, which company is this?' And when Manjusha told him, he swatted the problem away. It wasn't even a problem. 'Sonica? *Arre*, I know Kapoor, Vineet Kapoor, owner of Sonica. Many years ago we used to play cricket together. *Bada tagda yaar tha mera but hum touch mein nahin rahe* (He was a great friend of mine but we haven't kept in touch.) You have his number? Please give me his number.'

'No, Mr Ramani, I don't have the owner's number, but I do have the number for the A&R Manager at Sonica, Pratap Singh Jhala. If you like, I can give it to you,' Manjusha offered.

'*Jhalla?*' Ramani guffawed loudly, distorting Jhala's name to make it sound like the Punjabi word for an idiot. '*Jhalla?*' he repeated and soon he was in splits, his laughter like helpless braying. Manjusha found this in very poor taste, also very childish, but she waited silently for Ramani to stop being an ass. The braying finally stopped. Manjusha imagined the man wiping his eyes before he resumed the conversation. This time, Ramani had another proposition, '*Achha*, if copyright-shopyright is with Sonica, why take tension and waste our time, Manjusha ji? You can record the songs for us again. I mean, these are all traditional songs, *hai na? Licence-vicence ka koi jhanjhat hi nahin*! (No hassle of licence at all!)'

Yes, she probably could record the songs again, Manjusha told herself, but she had better be smart and clarify everything right at the start. She remembered an incident from two years ago, when a lady film-maker working on a documentary on dowry deaths and domestic violence had approached her and asked her for a song for the opening credits. Moved by the stories of the women featured in the documentary, Manjusha had agreed to compose and sing pro bono—the film-maker claimed she had no funding; no one was willing to finance such a 'depressing' project which 'tarnished India's image'. Determined to help, not only did Manjusha not charge the lady a single paisa, she also helped negotiate discounted terms with the studio and sessions musicians. But once the recording was completed and handed over, the film-maker vanished without so much as a thank you. Barely a month later, she released the film without even sending Manjusha an invitation for the screening. Worse, she sold the song to a production house making a television chat show on celebrity women. No permission was sought from Manjusha, nor was she offered any money. As if this wasn't bad enough, the chat show did not acknowledge Manjusha as the composer-singer, and only thanked the lady film-maker for permission to use the song. Outraged, Manjusha had contemplated legal action, but even as she tried to get an idea of the cost of litigation, the lady film-maker flew off to the United Kingdom to marry a knighted gentleman of Indian origin. Faced with the prospect of getting the lady to respond from overseas, Manjusha abandoned the idea of a legal remedy. But she had promised herself she would not let it happen again. Maybe now was the time to fulfil that promise.

Before she knew it, Manjusha heard herself saying confidently, 'Yes, Mr Ramani, I can re-record the songs with a different arrangement. But I also collected hundreds of other wedding songs during my research for that project which I could not use. I can sing some of those for your film. But I have a few questions. Who is composing the music for your film, and who will be given the credit for these songs? And what will I be paid for giving you the songs and recording them for you?'

Ramani replied, 'Music for all my films has been composed by Rukkesh-Nurresh, everyone knows that. Music for *Dil Pardesi* will also be by them. And credit for music and the songs will also be given to them. Your name will be in playback.'

Manjusha was nervous about offending Ramani if she pursued the matter any further. After all, it wasn't every day that a classical artiste like herself was approached by a Bollywood film-maker to sing for a blockbuster film. But neither could she resign herself to letting Rakesh-Naresh take credit for songs they had neither heard of nor composed. They would do it without fear or compunction, even if they didn't have Raj Ramani to hide behind, because this kind of thing was not at all uncommon in their profession. She knew of several instances of exploitation and appropriation; far too many people in the film industry routinely stole entire tunes, lyrics, compositions, ideas and more, because they knew they could get away smoothly with the theft. They would even hold forth in interviews on how the song had come to them in a dream one night, and they had woken up the next morning with the complete lyrics, interludes and arrangements in their head and on their lips! What the hell, she told herself, she wasn't going to be conned again. She had better get this out of the way. Bracing for battle, she told Ramani:

'Yes, Mr Ramani. I know that Rakesh-Naresh have scored for all your films and have given you some big hits. In fact, it will be a privilege to work with them. But you will appreciate that these songs that I record are not composed by them. Or by me, for that matter. Therefore, the credit should say something like this: So and so song: from the traditional wedding repertoire of North India; researched, sourced and performed by Manjusha Saxena, and arranged by Rakesh-Naresh.'

There was silence once again on the other end of the line. This time, some laboured breathing, too, as if

Ramani was trying very hard not to explode. He seemed to have finally realized that he was speaking to someone who was a professional, too much of a professional, in fact. She would not be taken in by a sweet-talking Bollywood celebrity. Well, then, it was time for some plain speaking. These classical musicians could be bloody pests, he had heard. They thought no end of themselves. And this one seemed to be well informed about rights and legalities too. He would have to use a strong dose of a different kind of medicine with this woman, he thought. His tone changed from pleasant to cold.

'Look, madam ji,' he began, 'I have recorded all kinds of songs. I have recorded traditional songs as well, with the greatest singers from India and Pakistan. Do you remember, in *Yaara Dildara* I got the great Pakistani star Jameela Sheikh to sing a Punjabi folk song? It was a mega-hit and topped all the charts for months. Well, Jameela Sheikh was famous for that song, and we got her to sing it for my film, but Rakesh-Naresh got the credit for it, and she was acknowledged for performing the song. I have so many other examples I can give you, so don't worry about credits. But...' Here he allowed a dramatic pause, and when he spoke again, his voice was pure steel. 'But you talked about payment. No one talks to Raj Ramani about payment. No one, not even the stars. Who do you consider a star in the music industry? Name the biggest playback star you have heard of.'

Manjusha immediately reeled off the names of playback greats who had held sway over the music industry for decades. Ramani dismissed them all rudely: 'Oh forget them! Expiry date *maal*. No one calls them anymore. Let me tell you that today's stars, Sarika, Savita, Shankar, Sikandar—all of them were given their big breaks by me. I repeat: by me! And they were grateful that I gave them a break. They never asked me for a *naya paisa*. Even today, I pay them nothing more than five thousand or ten thousand rupees maximum. You must have heard of Miss Sargam—she was a pop star and she was a classical star, you know that. She was versatile, and you will not like to hear this but she was—she is—even bigger than you. And who gave Miss Sargam her biggest film hits? Yours truly. She was talented, I made her sexy. She sang all those songs free for me, and if she hadn't taken retirement, I would not be making phone calls to you, my dear madam. But I have no ego. I like your wedding songs and you deserve a good break. But if you think that you are going to sing for a Bollywood film and earn lakhs, forget it. You will be singing for Raj Ramani and he does not pay anyone that kind of money. He makes stars, he gives them stardom. Now, tell me, are you ready or not?'

Manjusha was livid, her ears and face burning with humiliation. She felt for a moment that she would choke with anger, but once again she braced herself and said in an equally steely tone—a tone she hadn't known she was capable of: 'Mr Ramani. Have you said what you wanted to say?'

When Ramani answered in the affirmative, she continued, 'Then please listen carefully to what *I* have to say. It was you who approached me and invited me to sing for you, because you felt that you would like to feature my work in your film. I did not grovel at your feet for a break. Did I?'

Although she heard Ramani say no, she carried on as if she hadn't: 'Since I did not ask you for any favour, you should be aware that you have approached a professional. If you want me to sing in your film, it will be on terms and conditions that are acceptable to both of us and you will need to pay me my professional fee, whatever that may be. As for your claim about giving breaks to successful singers and making them stars, you are arrogant and delusional. You cannot make anyone a star, certainly not me. It is the hard work of my gurus, my own crazy obsession with music and some amount of talent that may or may not make me a star. You are welcome to go looking for fabulous Miss Sargam—and she *is* fabulous, but no thanks to you. I have no wish to sing for someone as crude as you, Mr Ramani, so don't ever, *ever* call me again.'

She put the receiver firmly back on its cradle and sat back, flushed and trembling a little, but satisfied with her response.

As Manjusha had expected, she did not hear from Raj Ramani again. Six months later, *Dil Pardesi* was released with greater than usual fanfare and publicity. The stars from the film went on an aggressive PR drive, reading out the prime-time news on one television channel, advising people on financial investments on another channel, making appearances on every chat show, reality show, dance contest, talent contest. The publicity campaign for Ramani's film virtually took over the print and television media for a fortnight. *Dil Pardesi* opened to full houses and earned crores, with the music topping all charts. A few weeks after its launch, Manjusha decided to go and see the film. As the opening credits rolled and the background score started playing, she heard several of the songs she had recorded for the wedding song album set. They had been sung by a raucous-voiced female singer pretending to be a 'folk singer', and altered slightly in text or melody. After all, they were 'traditional' songs and could be sung by anyone. But the credit for the music, naturally, went to 'Rukkesh-Nurresh'.

At the Feet of His Master

'Where've you reached, bro?' Sharad had his hands on the steering wheel and his phone tucked between his shoulder and ear as he parked his car by the side of the road. 'Okay,' he said, to the man on the other end, 'I'll go down to the studio, come straight there. See ya.'

He got out of the car, slipped the car keys into his pocket, opened the gate that led to a three-storey house in Ghaziabad, on the outskirts of Delhi, and made his way to the basement, towards what must be the tiniest of control rooms any sound studio could have.

Crammed into this basement studio were a computer table, a chair and an old and rotting cane seat on which two people could sit side by side, provided they weren't generously proportioned. On the table were ranged the bare necessities for a home studio: a desktop processor and a screen that was almost too large for the room, a keyboard and mouse, and two Genelec studio monitors.

Between the nano, makeshift control room and the studio floor that was only marginally larger, was a wooden partition with a glass pane. Propped against the pane was a small acrylic idol of Lord Ganapati, with pink ears, orange turban, rosy cheeks and glitter on tusk and forehead, and next to it, the metal head of a popular godwoman with a glittering Om rising from the forehead. Facing the computer and the deities sat a short, tubby man, about thirty-five years of age, bald, fair and neatly dressed in blue denim trousers and a checked blue shirt. His gleaming forehead bore the faint mark of an orange tilak, acquired either during his morning prayer ritual or perhaps from a visit to a temple on his way to work.

Sharad greeted him with a jovial 'Namaste, Pandit ji. *Kya haal chaal?* (How's is going?)'

'Namaste, Namaste, *Bhaisaab*,' answered Pandit ji softly. 'You should tell me about yourself. *Hamara kya, wohi daal roti ke chakkaron men phanse rehte hain.* (Nothing new here, the same old grind to earn a living.) Some chai?'

He disappeared from the room to arrange for tea, and Sharad lowered himself gingerly into the cane seat, casting an amused and slightly disdainful eye around the little studio.

Pandit ji was, in fact, Shivendra Kumar Jha from Bihar, formerly a music teacher in a municipal school in Chhapra who perforce had to move to Delhi when he was not paid his salary for six months. In debt, and anxious to provide for his family of ageing parents, a young wife and a little son, he had thought Delhi might provide some work as a teacher or professional singer. But after a long and tiring struggle, he chose to surrender at the feet of Shri Vatsalyamai Mata, a godwoman whose reputation as the very epitome of compassion, mercy and wisdom had gathered such momentum in just a few years that along with lakhs of disciples, she now had a sprawling ashram in Punjab with branches in the major metro cities, besides several sub-offices of the businesses she owned, from a chain of pure vegetarian dhabas to a fleet of buses to ferry pilgrims to temples, gurdwaras and dargahs across North India. A Bihari friend who was Shri Mata ji's disciple had happened to bump into Shivendra one evening when, by happy coincidence, both men had chosen the India Gate lawns for a family outing. With a little help from his fellow Bihari, Shivendra managed to secure an introduction to one of Shri Mata ji's *sewaks*, one of hundreds of men and women who had dedicated their lives to her service. The *sewak* was organizing a *pravachan*, a sermon, by Mata ji at the Ramlila Grounds in Delhi. A singer was required for the event, and Shivendra found himself offering his services in the hope of networking and securing potential clients from among the masses that were expected to gather at the grounds. As luck would have it, Shri Mata ji took a shine to the earnest young singer, and as he prostrated himself before her after the *pravachan*, resting his forehead on her feet, she declared, 'Come to the ashram on Monday. Let us see what we can do for you.'

Monday shone brightly on Shivendra: Shri Mata ji directed her aides to hire him as the lead singer for a music group she wanted to retain on a permanent basis, to accompany her for the many *pravachans* and *kathas* she was invited to deliver to the ever-growing numbers of her followers. He would head her music team, and in return get basic accommodation at one of the many properties she owned, a monthly retainer and a fee for each of the events in which he performed. He would also be paid a small fee for each of the albums he created for the ashram. With prior permission, he could also rent out the in-house studio at the ashram to non-ashramites and work with them, provided his activities did not interfere with anything that Shri Mata ji planned.

The arrangement worked perfectly for Shivendra and he remained true to the terms offered to him. Only when Shri Mata ji's schedule allowed him some free time would he take up other assignments—working occasionally as a music director for Bhojpuri films and private albums, and at times assisting electronic music artistes and DJs who wanted to include an element of traditional Indian music in their tracks. Gabbar n Mak, the famous electronic dance music duo, were his regular collaborators and often came to him seeking advice, tunes, and the odd dollop of Indian music as and when they required such a dose to 'give a twist' to their compositions.

By the time Shivendra returned bearing a tray with a flask of hot tea, disposable glasses and a saucer with some biscuits arranged on it, a freshly showered and cologned Mayur was also ensconced in the tiny studio. Together, Mayur and Sharad formed the popular Gabbar n Mak duo. Both were about the same age as Shivendra, and affluent, well-read, well-travelled and considered pioneers of sorts in India by virtue of being two of the earliest electronic music artistes in the country. Both worked hard and partied even harder. They also pursued parallel professions: Sharad, who was Gabbar, tended to his father's succesful construction business during the day, and Mayur—Mak—worked as a freelance music composer, programmer and producer for several ad agencies. But their true and lasting passion was EDM, and their partnership was an enduring one. For the last decade or so, Gabbar n Mak had played hundreds of succesful gigs armed with their laptops, headphones and a steady stream of guest artistes, making millions dance to their music. On each of their many albums, at least one track or significant components of several tracks featured contributions by Shivendra Kumar. The duo referred to him as 'Pandit ji' in deference to his knowledge of Hindustani classical and North-Indian folk music and of Hindi and Urdu poetry.

It was Pandit ji who had suggested that they include up-tempo Rajasthani folk songs in their award-winning album *Dune Tune Desserts*. The 'Pallo latkay' track sung for them by the gravel-voiced Reshma Rathod, a young singer from Jaisalmer, became a huge hit when the album was released some years ago. Both the song and the singer were Pandit ji's discoveries, and today Gabbar n Mak hoped to persuade their old buddy to dig up another stunner.

Once tea and biscuits had been served and consumed, small talk over and done with, Sharad took the lead, casually brushing biscuit crumbs off his black T-shirt as he said: '*Achha* Pandit ji, we need your help on a track we are producing. It's for a big Hollywood movie. Have you heard of—you must have heard of her...Naina Nagpal?'

Shivendra, always a straightforward, transparent man, made no attempt to conceal his ignorance. '*Aap toh jaante hain bhaisaab, hum chhoti jagah ke chhote aadmi hain. Bahut kuchh nahin jaante.* (You know well, bhai sahab, I'm a small man from a small place. There's a lot that I don't know.)'

'*Kya baat karte hain Pandit ji* (What are you saying, Pandit ji),' Sharad protested. '*Jo aap jaante hain woh hum jaise log sau saal mein nahin seekh payenge. Genius hain aap, sharminda mat keejiye. Khair, Naina ji Hollywood mein bada naam hain.* (People like us can try for a hundred years but we won't acquire the knowledge you have. You're a genius, don't embarrass us. Anyway, this Naina ji is a big name in Hollywood.) She's a film director, her last film was in the running for an Oscar. She's Indian, but lives and works in the US. She's making a new movie and she has asked us to work on the soundtrack, and we would really like you to work with us on the most important tracks. So you see, the film is based on the true life story of two boys, one Afghan and the other from India, both from very poor homes. Both are sold to a wealthy Afghan *bacha baaz* as *bacha bereesh*—you know, young boys who dress up as women and dance to entertain men. It's a tradition there. But they don't just dance, they're also sexually abused... Now, these two young boys are friends but they also try to outdo each other in pleasing their owner. The young Indian boy, just twelve years old, submits to his owner's sexual slavery without any resistance. In one scene, the boy is passed around among guests attending a party organized by his master, and Naina wants a song that will make a powerful statement. She wants a Hindi song, something strong and earthy. You know we always come to you for such a requirement. What we're looking for is a track that has a party mood—like 'Pallo latkay', *yaad hai na?*—but also conveys the tragedy of the boy's story and exploitation. Boss yaar, you have to help us with this, you're the only one who can do this.'

Shivendra looked decidedly shocked at what he had just heard. Stories of slavery, exploitation, violence and debauchery were not unknown to him, but this *bacha baazi* tradition was unfamiliar, and he was astounded that someone wanted to make a movie about it. It didn't seem right...He had initially been excited about scoring with Gabbar n Mak for a Hollywood movie, but now he wasn't so sure.

'*Baap re, Sharad bhai! Aisi khaufnaak situation mein gaanaa?* (My God, Sharad bhai! A song in such a horrific situation?)'

'But that's the whole point, boss,' countered Mayur. 'Don't you see? Creating a contrast with the music will really heighten the sense of tragedy. *Aap gaanaa to socho,* and then we can decide whether or not it will work in the situation.'

'*Bhai,* on the spur of the moment I can't think of any song for this situation. *Yeh toh kuchbh alag hi maamla hai* (This is something else altogether),' said Shivendra. 'But give me some time and I'll see if I can come up with something or not, okay?'

'We don't have too much time, Pandit ji,' urged Sharad, 'Give it a try, please.'

Mayur leaned forward and said, 'Please, boss. *Hollywood ka chance hai hum sab ke liye. Aur bada important subject hai, yeh film duniya ko hila degi.* (It's a chance at Hollywood for all of us. And it's a very important subject, this film will shake up the world.)'

Shivendra gave in. '*Theek hai, aap befikr raho, main kuchh karta hoon* (Okay, don't worry, I'll manage something),' he reassured them.

Sharad and Mayur prepared to bring the meeting to a close, but Shivendra still had something to say. Very tentatively and with some trepidation, he cleared his throat and began hesitantly, '*Ek baat aur hai. Pata nahi aap donon se kehna bhi chahiye ki nahin, par ab dimaagh mein aa hi gayi hai toh keh deta hoon.* (There's one more thing. I don't know if I should even bring it up with the two of you, but now that it's on my mind, I may as well make a clean breast of it.) You see, I've done so many songs with both of you—"Pallo latkay", "Awara", "Deewane", and so many more. But no one really knows that I have had any role to play in creating these songs because—*woh kya kehte hain—haan,* credits...the credits never mention my name. This would never have occurred to me, you see...but then I noticed that in your last album you have mentioned everyone and thanked each and every person, including Ramu, the office boy at your studio—and you have even thanked your cats Bijli and Chamki, Sharad bhai. The only person who got no thanks, no mention, was me. Maybe you forgot...My wife also noticed it and mentioned it to me, but I told her it must have been an oversight. After all, you are like my brothers and you won't allow any injustice to be done. *Toh bhai logon, iss baar...zara dekh lena please* (So my brothers, this time... see to it, please).'

Now it was Gabbar n Mak's turn to be shocked, and they were silent for a few minutes, unable to either defend themselves or offer a plausible excuse. Finally, a trifle shame-faced, Sharad said cautiously, 'Really sorry, Pandit ji. Won't happen again. We'll make sure everything is to your satisfaction this time, promise. So when should we call? In a couple of days? Okay, *chalte hain*!'

Shivendra walked up the stairs and to the gate with them, then returned to the studio and tidied it meticulously before he locked up and left for the day.

A week later, the three met again at the studio. Shivendra had asked for the meeting because he thought he had a song that might work for them.

'*Bhai logon*,' he began in his soft-spoken manner, 'you might want to use some old-style poetry for this song. You know, there are these lines from a much longer poem which you could use in those scenes where this poor boy is being passed from one drunken *bacha baaz* to the other: "*Jin bheshya mharo sahab rijhe, sohi bhesh dharungi.*"'

Gabbar n Mak looked blank, so he translated into modern Hindi: 'I will dress in whatever manner pleases my master. That's what the line says.'

'*Rocking*, dude! Yaar, you're such a star,' said Mayur in delight. 'I was sure you'd come up with something, but *iss baar toh...yaar, yaar...*' and he leaned forward, grabbed Shivendra's face in both hands and kissed him on the forehead. 'You've completely nailed it!'

'Really?' asked a beaming Shivendra. 'So you see, this is from a much longer poem by Meerabai—*Bala main bairaagan hoongi*...But I thought this particular line would be really suitable.'

'Okay,' Sharad chimed in. 'So these are Meerabai's lyrics, right? Then they'll be in the public domain. Good! *Copyright-shopyright ka lafdaa bhi nahi hoga.* (There'll be no copyright hassle.) Excellent! But for the album we should do the full song and not just this line. *Hai na?*'

The three men huddled together in the small room, clustered around the desktop with Pandit ji in command and Gabbar n Mak peering anxiously over his shoulder, creating a scratch recording to send to Naina.

'Tempo?' Shivendra asked. '150 bpm okay?'

Before he could go any further Sharad interjected,

'You must have some of those loops we sent you for "Deewane". Why don't we just try and use one of those for now?'

Shivendra promptly located a folder on his machine titled 'GM' for Gabbar n Mak, found the loops, and began to play them. Sharad identified one that he felt might work and Shivendra seconded his selection. He transferred the file to a new folder. Excited and eager, the three worked intensely with occasional tea and cigarette breaks, and within a few hours they were ready with a demo track in Shivendra's voice. As they listened carefully, Sharad complimented Shivendra on his singing: 'Boss, this is awesome. Your voice sounds very moving and I think Naina's going to ask you to dub the final yourself. So, Pandit ji, direct Hollywood?'

Pleased as punch with the compliment, and the possibility of singing for a mega-budget Hollywood film, Shivendra beamed quietly as his two collaborators ribbed him about becoming an international singing sensation. And within minutes Gabbar n Mak's joking and leg-pulling had ignited a latent aspiration in Shivendra's heart—of moving ahead from his fairly comfortable but monotonous existence to a life of fame, acclaim and international success. Maybe he could even become an overseas citizen with Mata ji's blessings. After all, she was working on opening ashrams in the US and UK. Who knew, she might even make the shift for him easier, and then he could send his son to school in America, while he became a star in Hollywood! And then, maybe, perhaps, an Oscar...His heart began to bang against his ribs.

Many of Shivendra's dreams and hopes were embedded in the recording that Gabbar n Mak finally sent to Naina Nagpal a couple of days later. Naina loved the demo track, fell in love with Shivendra's voice, and refused to consider any other singer for the final version. No amount of advice and suggestions from her marketing team—which was of the opinion that a well-known playback voice from Pakistan or India would give them an edge when negotiating audio rights—would make her change her mind. There was something in Shivendra's voice, she felt, something that went straight to the heart, like a flaming arrow. When her marketing team persisted, she put her foot down.

'I'm going to use my veto, guys,' she said. 'He's the man. We won't replace his voice.'

And so it was that Shivendra dubbed the final version of the song, which was to appear in the album in two versions—the original titled 'At the feet of my master' and the second version titled 'At the feet of my master (Reprise)'. Shivendra was paid handsomely, but of course not for two tracks, only one. 'But then,' he said to himself without any rancour, 'it was just the one song, not really two different tracks.' He had dubbed one track, the original, with four lines from the Meerabai bhajan, or devotional song, and the reprise version included the complete bhajan and was therefore a longer track. Splitting the entire track into two different versions and calling the second one 'unplugged', 'reprise' or whatever was just a marketing gimmick, and a way of getting a respectable album length, he understood that. From his point of view, he had put in time, effort and skill into a single track, so it was all right not to be paid extra.

He was pleased with the way the song worked out, and the sense of satisfaction lingered for several weeks after the track was finalized and taken to the UK for mastering by Gabbar n Mak. On their return, when he heard the mastered track, he felt once again that they hadn't done too badly. There was something quite unique about the song. Left to his own devices, he might have turned it into a more conventional bhajan in the popular style, with xylophones and manjiras, a flute and a chorus. But he had to admit Gabbar n Mak had brought a special touch to the arrangement, cushioning it with lush string arrangements (recorded, he was told, in Hungary). They later brought in a double bass player from the USA to dub the track at their own studio, and added majestic *alaaps* on the sarangi. What emerged was a beautifully recorded track that the creators could be proud of. It now remained to be seen whether or not it would work with the film.

It was almost a year before the film was finally ready. Another few months went by while the promos were created, and finally Sharad called to inform Shivendra that the music launch would probably take place in late April or early May, just before the film was released in June. Worried that the launch date could clash with one of Mata ji's *satsangs* where his presence was mandatory, Shivendra sought audience with Mata ji. He was granted *darshan* within the week and duly presented himself, wife Sunita by his side, both carrying boxes of *mithai*, marigold garlands, a blingy gota-tacked saree in pillar-box red, and a matching red shawl with zari embroidery as gifts.

Mataji's *darshan* hall was, as always, air-conditioned and scented with sandalwood essence. But the waiting area, packed with devotees eager to seek the benediction of their Divine Mother, reeked of sweat and was like the inside of an enormous *tandoor*, the ceiling and pedestal fans providing very little relief. Volunteers dressed in magenta T-shirts with Mata ji's photograph digitally printed on the front, and '*Ma hum tere dulaare*' ('Mother, we are your darlings') emblazoned on the back, herded visitors efficiently into four rows, directing the crowds in as orderly a manner as was possible. Shivendra did not have to join any of the lines, and was whisked into

Mata ji's presence in just under ten minutes. Seated on a huge silver throne, her bare feet placed on a velvet footstool, she was resplendent in a rose-pink silk sari with an intricate lace edging sent by a devotee from Spain. The colour of the sari complemented her peaches-and-cream complexion. On her radiant forehead, below a silver band with an Om mounted on it, she wore a sandalwood tilak, and around her neck was a garland of the finest orchids flown in from Thailand by an ardent follower. A Rolex watch and a huge dazzling ruby on her right hand completed her costume for the day. Her daily rose-petal and milk manicure and pedicure ensured her hands and feet were soft as a baby's bottom and the colour of a fresh rosebud.

It was at these soft and pink feet that Shivendra and spouse now knelt, and then bent forward to touch their foreheads to Mataji's toes, the nails painted the exact colour and shade of her sari. They remained frozen in this position as Mata ji blessed them following her usual ritual. Holding her palms about a foot away from their heads, she closed her eyes and went into a trance of sorts. At some point she opened her eyes, turned them upwards until the eyeballs could no longer be seen and only the whites gleamed terrifyingly. Then she worked her finger-tips as if she were sprinkling something on the devotees at her feet for about half a minute. Finally, she opened her eyes, flashed a wide smile and yelled, '*Chamatkaar*! (Miracle!)' The devoted couple sat up and laid their gifts near her feet and immediately two attendants sprang up to gather the boxes and garlands and put them away. Shivendra and Sunita now stood before Mata ji, hands folded and waiting to receive a signal to speak. Mata ji looked on fondly, beaming away and examining them closely, before she suddenly said, '*Aa jo, aa jo puttar, Mata ji ke paas aa jo.* (Come here, come, my children, come to your Mother.)' Both the *puttars* went closer and sat down obediently at her feet, one on either side of the throne, looking up at her like adoring puppies. Once she had asked them how they were doing and they had duly acknowledged that all was well with them, thanks to her blessings, Shivendra asked if he could take a minute of her time. His wish was granted and he told her, in a rush, that he had composed and sung a track for a Hollywood movie, '*aap ke ashirwaad se* (with your blessings)'.

Mata ji smiled, and turning to her attendants, said, 'I had told you, hadn't I, that he would go far? Believe your mother now?'

As she turned her attention back to Shivendra, he asked, 'Mata ji, if you permit, may I go for the album launch if it happens in Delhi?'

'Of course you must,' said Mata ji in mock surprise. 'Look at this silly fellow, asking if he should go or not!

Of course you have to go. Your Mata ji will be very angry, *bacche*, if you don't go. What could please a mother more than seeing her children get fame and acclaim? After all, a mother's pleasure lies in her children's happiness.'

Shivendra was so relieved to hear this that he became dewy-eyed with gratitude, his lower lip quivered and he could not speak as his voice choked with emotion. He also noticed that the attendants were getting restive waiting for a signal to usher in the next devotee, so he quickly brushed his forehead once more against Mata ji's painted and varnished toe nails, and took his leave. His wife followed suit, and soon they were out of the ashram and flagging down an auto rickshaw to go home. Delighted with the way the meeting had gone, Shivendra felt a fierce sense of excitement. Something told him his new song would change his life. He quietly slipped an arm around his wife, drawing her closer as they rode home. Though more than a little surprised at this uncharacteristically romantic gesture, she did not question him and sat through the ride in companionable silence, happy for him.

The album was launched at the grand Taj Palace hotel on a Saturday evening. When they invited him to the launch, Gabbar n Mak had asked Shivendra to sing, or rather lip synch, to the track they had created. It was all very exciting, and in readiness, Shivendra embarked on a shopping trip to Karol Bagh, and returned with a new kurta ensemble for himself and an Anarkali outfit for his wife. Shivendra also rehearsed with the track to make sure he could lip synch convincingly. Finally, the big day arrived. One of Sunita's friends in the neighbourhood generously offered to baby-sit so that the couple could enjoy the special evening without having to worry about their little one. At exactly fifteen minutes to six—anxious not to be late, yet not too early—the couple hired a radio cab to ride to the launch dressed in their newly purchased finery.

But even as they disembarked at the porch and made their way into the enormous, glittering banquet hall of the Taj Palace, they realized that they looked shabby and out of place among the glitterati trickling in for the event. Designers, models, actors, journalists, corporate honchos, they were all there in droves and the bustle and dazzle quite overwhelmed the couple. As soon as she recognized a celebrity, Sunita would whisper excitedly to Shivendra, '*Suniye, ye woh TV anchor Sureeli hai na?* (Listen, isn't that the TV anchor Sureeli?)' or '*Arre dekhiye, ye toh woh cricketer Prince hai!* (Oh look, it's that cricketer, Prince!)'. Shivendra was used to seeing the rich and famous gather at Mata ji's court, but this gathering was a class apart. He hadn't seen anything like it before and he felt suddenly tongue-tied and out of place. Leaning towards Sunita, he said in awe, '*Neetu, hum yahan kya kar rahein hai?* (What are we doing here, Neetu?)', which made Sunita giggle nervously.

And then Gabbar n Mak were walking up to them. The two were in party spirits and greeted Shivendra boisterously, hugging him and poking fun at him for his smashing kurta ensemble. '*Pandit ji, chamak rahe ho aaj toh, kiski jaan loge…*(You look splendid, Pandit ji, who're you going to kill today…)' but as soon as they noticed that Sunita was also there, they became more respectful, greeting her with '*Bhabhi ji,* Namaste.' Sharad pulled at Shivendra's arm and said, 'Come, let's introduce you to Naina.' The foursome snaked their way through scattered groups of people nursing drinks and exchanging party chatter, till they reached an unusually dense cluster of photographers and media persons surrounding a lady whom Shivendra and Sunita recognized as Naina Nagpal from her photographs in magazines and her many television appearances. Making his way gradually but deftly though the shutterbugs, Sharad managed to catch Naina's eye and waved out to her. She responded with a cheerful wave and rushed forward to greet her music directors. The three exchanged hugs and kisses, and then Mayur turned towards Shivendra and Sunita and gestured to both to come forward.

'Naina, we'd like to introduce you to Shivendra, whose voice you loved so much, remember?'

Naina stood still for a moment, as Shivendra and Sunita came forward to meet her. Then she stretched out both arms and said, 'Hi, I just *have* to give you a hug! *Aap jaante nahin aapne apni khoobsurat awaaz se kitna rulaaya hai mujhe* (You don't know how much you've made me cry with your beautiful voice.)' She wrapped her arms around Shivendra and held him for several seconds, while he stood awkwardly, not sure how he should respond. As she released him from her bear-hug, she said, 'Thank you for that song, Shivendra, it's just stunning. My absolute favourite in the film.'

'Thank you, madam,' said Shivendra hesitantly, then turned to introduce her to Sunita who was standing shyly by his side. In a few minutes, Naina's assistant appeared to extricate her from the crowd and lead her to the stage erected in the far corner of the hall for the formal album release.

The stage had a busy backdrop of large posters and publicity stills from the film, as well as shots of Naina at work, and a portrait of Gabbar n Mak. Logos of a host of partners—media partners, PR partners, radio partners, hospitality partners, travel partners—were sprinkled generously on different parts of the backdrop. Partner brands that had put in large amounts of money into the film or its promotions were prominently acknowledged and their logos were displayed at strategic points on the posters. Meagre contributors were tucked away in the bottom corners where no one would notice them. A long table was placed centrestage with six name cards: Naina Nagpal, Gabbar, Mak, Mahesh Meghchandani (the producer), Abhay Raina (CEO, Alaap Music) and Changez Abidi (the Pakistani actor who had a major role in the film). A lectern was in place for the compere, a popular jockey with the film's radio partner. He emerged from the crowd, vaulted onto the stage deftly and took his position behind the microphone. Soon the launch of the music was underway, with short speeches by the six people on stage. Speeches done, the super six were presented gift-wrapped copies of the albums, which they unwrapped for the photo op. Camera shutters clicked crazily, flash bulbs sprayed bursts of light on the super six, and gigantic LED screens on either side of the stage played the promo for the film. Shivendra heard a snatch from 'At the feet of my master' for a few seconds, but then it disappeared as the promo hurtled on to its quick and imminent end. But it left Shivendra and Sunita with a tingle of anticipation. They looked at each other and smiled with delight before turning their attention back to the proceedings, in time to hear the compere asking 'the spectafabulous singer Shivendra Kumar' to join him on stage.

Shivendra made his way to the stage, a quiet,

unassuming and unlikely figure in the gathering of the rich and famous. He greeted the super six with a courteous namaste, then stood shyly to one side as the compere asked Naina Nagpal to present him with a copy of the album. As she presented the gift-wrapped album to Shivendra, the flash bulbs popped again and he bravely smiled and posed for them. There was no time to open the wrapping, because the compere was now asking him to please sing the track for the gathering. Gabbar n Mak pulled out their laptops and plugged in cables efficiently while a stagehand sprinted up to hand Shivendra a cordless mike. Signalling that they were ready, Gabbar n Mak played the track, one swinging his head from side to side along with the rhythm, the other swaying pendulum-like with the track. Sixteen bars into the track, Shivendra's voice gently slipped in, floating over the music initially and then soaring higher and higher. A hush descended over the gathering as his voice filled the room, though of course the occasional mobile phone still went off every now and then. Shivendra's singing, poignant to begin with, became disturbing as the track progressed, loaded with pain and agony and a devastating feeling of loss. Naina Nagpal could not stop her tears, and there were many in the audience who had lumps in their throats. Shivendra was unaware of the effect he was having on the audience, because he was concentrating on synching correctly with the song, intent on giving his best even though he wasn't actually singing. When the track ended, there was silence for a few seconds during which Shivendra shuffled and smiled awkwardly while Gabbar n Mak gave him a thumbs up, and then there was thunderous applause that did not die down for almost a minute. Naina rushed to Shivendra, hugged him and then declared in a voice choked with emotion, 'Ladies and gentlemen, my good friends Gabbar n Mak here have found a treasure in Shivendra Kumar. A big round of applause for the sublime Shivendra, please.'

Another enthusiastic round of applause followed, during which Shivendra smiled self-consciously, wondering if people could hear his heart beating as loudly as he could. Mercifully, the compere brought the ceremony to a close quickly and invited everyone for cocktails and snacks, urging them to have a 'rocking, fantabulous time'. People were back in party mode in an instant, with some headed to the bar to replenish their drinks, others smiling, waving at each other, exchanging small talk, and ogling slender young women in tiny black dresses and brawny young men in butt-hugging pants.

Shivendra got off the stage and walked through the hall towards Sunita, stopping occasionally to accept compliments. When he finally reached her, Shivendra offered the gift-wrapped album to his wife, and said, 'Open it.' She unwrapped the album, looked at the cover for a few seconds, turned it over to check the back cover, and found what she was looking for—her husband's name. Satisfied, she handed the unwrapped album to him, saying, '*Aap bhi dekhiye na.* (You look at it, too.)'

Shivendra checked the front cover cursorily, but it was the back cover with the credits that he looked at with greater interest. His name featured twice, as the singer for both versions of 'At the feet of my master'. But he could not find any acknowledgement of his role as composer and co-producer of the track. Perhaps it was mentioned in the detailed credits inside the booklet that went with the album. Yes, that was where it would be. But he couldn't possibly check that here, not in the middle of the party. It would be fine, he tried to tell himself. Nothing to worry about. If Gabbar or Mak had a problem giving him credit for the composition, they would have said so when he had brought up the matter during their first meeting for the project...But then, why wouldn't they put it on the back cover...No, he was being unduly suspicious. They must have had some compulsions which prevented them from insisting his name be carried on the back cover, along with their own. It must be in the booklet, they would have ensured that.

But try as he might, he could not discard altogether the niggling feeling that he had been duped once again, and he waited desperately for an opportune moment when he could leave the gathering, head home and go through the booklet carefully. By now he had lost all interest in the party and it took all the fortitude and patience he could muster to somehow hang around for half an hour, after which Sunita and he slipped out of the banquet hall, unnoticed by the revellers. In the lobby, he hurriedly fished out his phone from his kurta pocket to call for a radio cab. Fortunately, there were several cabs in the area and in a few minutes they were on their way home. In the cab, Shivendra asked Sunita to call their neighbours who were baby-sitting to inform them that they would be home in an hour. While Sunita made the call, Shivendra rested his head against the window, gazing out with brooding eyes. As soon as she hung up, Sunita asked, '*Kya hua?* (What's the matter?) Are you tired? You aren't feeling unwell, are you?' She put a hand on his forehead to check if he had a fever coming on.

Shivendra gestured with his right hand to reassure her but continued to look out as he said, 'Neetu, I think they've done it again. I can only see my name as singer on the album cover, not as composer and co-producer of the song. I'll only know for sure once I get home and check the booklet, I don't want to do it now, but I have a feeling they haven't kept their word. I hope I'm wrong, but if not, I'm not going to be silent this time. Enough is enough. Now leave me alone, Neetu, and don't fuss, please.'

They rode home in uneasy, troubled silence, which crept in with them as they unlocked the door to their flat and entered. While Sunita went to bring their son home, Shivendra rushed to their bedroom, where he pulled the booklet out of the album and flipped through the pages urgently till he found the page on which 'At the feet of my master' was mentioned. He scanned the credits repeatedly—lyrics, voice, strings, cello, bass, sarangi—but there was nothing about his role as composer and co-producer. He flipped through the remaining pages, and went to the section where Gabbar n Mak thanked Naina, the producer, their respective parents and families and pets. But not a word of thanks for him.

He sat on the edge of his bed, dejected and humiliated and wondering what to do next. He suddenly rushed towards the table in the room where he kept files, scores and other documents related to the projects he undertook. Scrambling around wildly among some loose papers, he fished out one that seemed to have what he was looking for. But in just a minute he put it back in the pile from which it had been extracted and returned to the edge of the bed, this time with his elbows resting on his knees and his head in his hands. The paper he had just checked was the only documentation he had about his involvement in the project, and all it contained was a receipt for 50,000 rupees, paid to him by Gabbar n Mak for 'voice dubbing of the track "At the feet of my master". For the sum of 50,000 rupees he had willingly surrendered all rights over the track. There was no legal contract; no agreement which described in detail his involvement in the track, and which assured him the right to be acknowledged as composer and co-producer. But then, he thought to himself, even if he had a contract what could he have done with it in this situation? He did not have the money to hire lawyers and fight a legal battle in India, or the US, perhaps, where Naina Nagpal lived. Sunita entered the room looking anxious but before she could ask him anything their eyes met, and Shivendra shook his head slowly to indicate that his hunch had been correct, he had been cheated again.

It was a restless night for Shivendra. He slept very little and woke up with a dull headache. But as soon as he got out of bed, he decided he would speak to Gabbar n Mak and ask for a clarification. Perhaps speaking his mind might rid him of the acute sense of betrayal, the abject dejection that sat like a stone in his heart. But it was no use hoping for a proper solution, he told himself the very next moment. He knew his collaborators to be suave, smooth-talking men who would come up with some clever explanation which would leave him with little option but to accept whatever story they spun.

Well, never mind. He would still call them. He could no longer let matters be. Enough was enough. He checked the time on his watch and realized it would be pointless calling either Gabbar or Mak before about one in the afternoon. Their phones would be switched off to allow them to sleep peacefully after all the hectic partying the night before. He waited impatiently for the hours to pass. Finally, at one sharp, he called Sharad but did not get through. He then tried Mayur's number, which also remained unanswered. In between, Sunita asked if he would like some lunch but he shook his head and said, 'Later, please.'

Finally, it was Sharad who called, at about three in the afternoon. His voice was still gruff from sleep, but he asked cordially: 'Did you call, Pandit ji?'

'Yes, I did,' answered Shivendra. His voice trembled a little as he steeled himself to speak his mind and continued, '*Aap ne zubaan di thi Sharad bhai.* (You had given me your word, Sharad bhai.) But you did it again. I did not expect this from the two of you, not after the conversation we had about acknowledging me for the composition.'

Sharad was wide awake now, and cut in saying, 'But the credit is there. Your name is there, isn't it, Pandit ji?'

'Don't pretend, Sharad bhai, please don't!' Shivendra's words tumbled out in a rush now and the tremor in his voice disappeared as he said angrily, 'I have only been acknowledged as the singer, not as the composer or the person who selected the lyrics, helped with the production and arrangement. Do you remember that I brought up this matter with you when you first came to speak to me about the track? You assured me that there would be no cause for complaint this time. And yet, it's the same story. The *same* old story. Why even bother to give me credit as a singer? You could just have said it was one of you who dubbed the track. *Dhokha hi dena tha toh itta sa bhi lihaaj kyun?* (If you'd decided to betray me, why make even this little concession?)'

Sharad tried to calm him down and said placatingly, 'Pandit ji, Pandit ji, please listen to me. Listen to me, please. This must be a printing error because I sent all the credits myself. Honestly. Please let me talk to Naina about this and we'll sort it out, okay?'

'Yes, yes,' countered Shivendra, 'I knew you would have some excuse to fob me off. What will you sort out now that the album is out? Don't think I'm a fool. You can't fool me any longer. You haven't acknowledged me on the album and I know it will be the same in the film. Remember, you will get what you deserve for being such cheats. Please don't try and explain anything to me. I'm done with you. Just leave me alone please, and don't bother to call again.'

He disconnected the call abruptly and sat down with

his head in his hands again, his eyes brimming with hot tears. A few minutes later, he rubbed his face with his palms almost as if to clear his head of all the anger and resentment. In control of his emotions, he called out to Sunita. 'Neetu, come let's have lunch. Sorry to have made you wait so long, but I just had to get this off my chest. *Chal*, let's eat.'

Mayur and Sharad tried to call Shivendra several times, but he did not take their calls or call back. He truly did not want to have anything more to do with them, and decided he would block them out forever from his life. He could have given them some sleepless nights if he had the money to hire a fancy lawyer and sue them just before the release of the movie. But he knew that he neither had the money nor the aggression and resilience to fight them legally, or to fight them in any way at all. Actually, he had surprised himself by speaking to Sharad as sharply as he had done. But it was over now, he told himself, no more thinking of them. It would only make him bitter and frustrated and poison his existence. He turned his attention back to his work: his projects with Shri Mata ji, his Bhojpuri albums of Kanwad bhajans and Chhat Puja songs. Above all, he concentrated on being the breadwinner for his family. He was almost grateful now for the comfortable monotony of his life. No dreams, no heartbreak. He would live by this rule. Simple.

Except that it wasn't quite so simple. He had wiped the memory of the experience from his mind. But the song would not be erased.

A couple of months into Shivendra's heartbreak, the film released worldwide with all the fanfare and publicity common for a big banner Hollywood release, particularly one by as prominent a director as Naina Nagpal. Being of Indian origin, her films always attracted immense media attention in India, and every day now there was some interview or feature or report about her new film. Try as he might, Shivendra could not avoid reports about the film and its signature song, and now and again he was made to relive the pain, anger and hurt he had experienced. Should he even try to see the movie? Just to establish beyond doubt if those two villains were really the shameless thieves they were? If the credits were absent from the film as well, he would be proved right. He decided he would take a call once the film released, but by the time the promos started on television and he heard his voice in the soundtrack, he had more or less made up his mind to buy a ticket for one of the shows in a neighbouring theatre.

As it happened, he did not have to buy that ticket. Because a day after the film had its India release, all hell broke loose. The dreaded HSSV, or Hindu Sanskriti Sewak Vahini, a militant right-wing group active in several parts of the country, decided that a Meerabai bhajan playing over a sequence where a boy was used as a sex slave was an intolerable insult to Hindu sentiments. It deserved a fitting response, which naturally could only be arson and violence at theatres which screened the film. Soon an FIR was filed against Naina, as well as Gabbar n Mak, and HSSV workers asked for an immediate and absolute ban on the film and life imprisonment for the filmmaker and music directors. When Gabbar reached the police station for questioning, irate HSSV workers pelted him with stones and sticks, injuring him and missing his eye by a hair's breadth. Outside theatres, effigies of Naina and Gabbar n Mak were burnt and stamped upon, and for a week primetime on news channels was devoted to shrill debates about the film and the protests. Shivendra could not ignore the controversy or pretend that he was unaffected by it. For a while, he felt that Gabbar n Mak had been served right for their duplicity, but when a television report showed a bleeding Gabbar being escorted to the hospital by police constables, his heart melted and he could barely stop himself from calling 'Sharad bhai' to express his sympathy. He quickly changed channels but there seemed to be no escaping the reports and noisy discussions around the film and the controversy.

The song was on every channel, and one evening Shivendra was stunned to hear his own name on a news programme—he was being identified as the singer who had not just lent his voice to the song, but also selected the poetry for it. Mayur, the as-yet uninjured half of Gabbar n Mak, was a panelist on the show and was describing at length the making of the song and how 'Shivendra Kumar Jha' had hit upon the idea of the Meerabai poem. Another panelist, a murderous looking HSSV office-bearer, was glaring at Mayur and suddenly snarled at him: 'Don't you try to wriggle out of the situation! You are the music directors for this film and you should have had better sense than to insult Hindu sentiments. I think you did it on purpose. You are anti-nationals! Hindu haters! Would you do something like this with an Islamic song, a Christian song? Would you, *hain*? You must apologize and give a written undertaking that you will never use any Hindu poem in your music without our clearance. And this film must be banned or Meera ji's bhajan removed from it. As for this Shivendra Kumar fellow, we will find him and if he has any hand in this, he will also be taught a proper lesson.'

Shivendra froze, terrified for his own safety, and that of his family. He quickly called out to Sunita and told her of the calamity. He would send her home to his parents with their son, where they would probably be safer than in Delhi, he said; she shouldn't call him from there, she should lie low; she should deny all knowledge of the song; she shouldn't worry, he would join them in Chhapra soon, as soon as he got permission from Mata ji…

As he babbled on, it was Sunita who came up with a solution, at least for the time being. '*Suniye, suniye toh*,' she said to stop him and then suggested they all take refuge with Shri Mata ji in her ashram. There could be no safer place for them at this time. Shivendra hugged her and almost wept in relief. While she packed a suitcase for the three of them, he called the ashram, asked to speak to Shri Mata ji's aides and hurriedly explained the situation to them. They said they would discuss the matter with Mata ji and let him know what to do. In about ten minutes he received a call with news that Mata ji had summoned him to the ashram with his family. Relieved, he called a cab and soon they were on their way. At the ashram, they were assigned a guest room for the night, and were told that Mata ji would meet Shivendra in the morning at seven. He was to be ready for the meeting.

Exactly at seven the next morning, a pale-looking Shivendra walked in to rest his head on Shri Mata ji's feet. She looked sombre, and as he bowed his head, she rolled up the newspaper she was reading and rapped him on the head with it. '*Khotta hai tu?* (Are you a donkey?),' she said sharply. 'Have you no brains, doing something like this in this day and age? Have I not taught you to be more careful? Now tell me how all this happened. And don't leave out any detail or I will be very angry with you. *Chal ab utth aur sach bol.* (Now get up and speak the truth.)'

Shame-faced and frightened, Shivendra blurted out the entire story to her bit by bit. Including the part about having been duped by Gabbar n Mak. When he finished, she asked, 'Where is the album?'

He said he had left it at home.

She signalled to a minion sitting to her right and as he bent his head and folded his hands, said: 'Get the album for me in the next half hour. I need it fast, understand? And send someone to get a copy of the film from somewhere. I want to see it and check if this donkey has been given credit for the composition.'

The minion rose to go, then stopped, half turned, bowed low at the waist and said, '*Lekin Mata ji, film par toh suna hai ban lag gaya hai.* (But Mata ji, I hear the film has been banned.)'

For which remark he received a whack on his bottom with the rolled-up newspaper. '*Ban se mujhe kya matlab?* (How does the ban matter to me?) Go get the film from someone. I don't care how.'

By the evening, Shri Mata ji had completed her investigation and Shivendra was summoned in her presence once again. 'Sit down,' she ordered. He sat at her feet, and hung his head in shame and remorse.

'Tomorrow morning I am going to call some media people and explain to them that you are one of my most religious and obedient disciples. You have only sung the song, you had no hand in composing it or selecting the lyrics. How could you even know that it would be used in such an ugly manner? You were not told anything about the film or the scene. You sang a bhajan because you are a very religious man, you thought you were singing it for a devotional film. This is what I will say. And you must not open your mouth. Do not talk to anyone and let me do the talking, do you understand?' She looked at the speechless man at her feet. '*Suna toone, khotte?* (Have you heard me, you donkey?)'

Shivendra nodded in relief and with a quivering voice tried to thank Mata ji. She stopped him short. 'Shut up now and do as I say. Not just this time but all your life. Let me handle this. Now go, you are safe here. Tell your wife also not to worry.'

By the evening of the following day, the stories that Shri Mata ji had planted started appearing on a few television channels and online sites and in the newspapers, establishing Shivendra's innocence and absolving him of any role in the controversial track other than having lent his voice to it.

In a couple of months, the uproar died down. Shivendra went back to his normal routine. Gabbar n Mak continued to defend themselves in the case filed against them. A year passed, then another, and with time Shivendra himself came to believe that he had no role to play in the song other than lending his voice to it. He gave up producing Bhojpuri albums, singing jingles, collaborating with other artistes. He had no time; he was always and happily busy with Ashram work. Gradually he became Shri Mata ji's favourite *khotta,* her donkey disciple. He followed her everywhere. And at her *pravachans* and *satsangs,* he always sat at her feet; the lotus feet of his Master.

Acknowledgements

I could not have become a musician, or told a single story about Indian music, without the guiding hand of my great gurus who trained me with a generosity that I perhaps did not deserve. To Pandit Ramashreya Jha 'Ramrang', Pandit Vinay Chandra Maudgalya, Pandit Vasant Thakar, Pandit Jitendra Abhisheki, Pandit Kumar Gandharva and Smt. Naina Devi, I owe an undying debt of gratitude.

And I could not have written these stories without the encouragement and constant support of my husband Aneesh Pradhan, whose advice and guidance I constantly seek—with what must surely be irritating frequency! I cannot thank him enough for patiently giving me his ear and attention even as he worked tirelessly on his own book and other assignments.

My thanks to my literary agent Kanishka Gupta for representing me with such diligence, patience and promptness.

I'm deeply grateful to Ravi Singh and the team at Speaking Tiger for accepting my first attempt at fiction and making it part of such an illustrious list. Ravi's editing of my stories has added a lustre to them that I could not have achieved on my own.

My gratitude to my gurubhai and photographer Rajan Parrikar for generously permitting me to use the portrait he shot of me some years ago.

Several friends have read through initial drafts of some of my stories, or have allowed me to read to them, and provided valuable suggestions and information. For this I remain indebted to Kunal Ray, Nitin Joshi, Sudhir Nayak, Vandana Raghunandan and Srijan Mahajan.

And finally, I'm able to sing, teach, read, write, and laugh through all the ups and downs of life only because of my incredible family that is always by my side. Though my parents Jaya and Skand Gupt are not physically present, their memory continues to both guide and comfort me constantly. There is no way I could adequately thank my sister Ragini Pasricha, nephew Raghav Pasricha, and my son Dhaval Mudgal for their unconditional support and honest, sometimes brutal assessment of all my work. My father-in-law Late Vasant Pradhan, my mother-in-law Kisan Pradhan, sisters-in-law Nishita Mhatre and Deepti Pradhan, nephew-in-law Sushan Mhatre and his wife Mridula have each contributed vitally to my being able to tell these stories in which humour camouflages the inevitable sadness that often casts a shadow over the lives of artistes. I thank them with all my heart.

And thank you, Miss Sargam, for flitting through this collection and adding sparkle to it.